START A SMALL UK BUSINESS

BUSINESS PLANNING TOOLS TO TURN YOUR IDEAS INTO BUSINESS SUCCESS

PETER BALL &
SANDRA BROOKES

Copyright © 2021 by Peter Ball & Sandra Brookes
All rights reserved.

No part of this book may be reproduced or transmitted in any form or by any means, electronic or mechanical, including photocopying, recording, or by any information storage and retrieval system without the written permission of the author, except where permitted by law.

Interior Design by FormattedBooks.com

ISBN: 979-8-495-89892-9 (paperback)
ISBN: 979-8-754-96072-5 (hardback)

DISCLAIMER

The publisher and authors have made every effort to ensure that the information in this book was correct at the time of going to press. This publication is designed to provide accurate information in regard to the subject matter covered, but the publisher and authors can assume no responsibility for errors, inaccuracies, omissions, or any other inconsistencies herein and hereby disclaim any liability to any party for any loss, damage or disruption caused by errors or omissions whether such omissions result from negligence, accident, or another cause.

This publication is meant as a source of valuable information for the reader, however it is not meant as a substitute for direct personal assistance. If such a level of assistance is required, the services of a competent professional should be sought.

This book is dedicated to the memory of
our good friend and colleague,

Dianne Horne

who was to join us in our Bluebell Business venture, but sadly had to follow another route herself due to cancer. We will donate £1 for each book we sell to the Christie NHS Foundation Trust Manchester, who cared for her throughout her illness.

CONTENTS

Chapter 1: Brand You!—Developing your Brand 1

Chapter 2: Business Planning—Creating your Plan 11

Chapter 3: Market & Competitor Research—
            Finding your Customers! 21

Chapter 4: Marketing—Sales & Customer Service.....................44

Chapter 5: Personal Character & Skills Analysis
            (SWOC)—Analysing your Personal Skills
            and Abilities 55

Chapter 6: Financials - Personal Survival Budget—
            How much will you need to draw from
            your business?...68

Chapter 7: Cash Flow Forecasting—How much money
            will flow through your business?...............................73

Chapter 8: Make it Happen! 94

ACKNOWLEDGEMENTS

We decided to write this book at the start of 2020 as the Covid 19 pandemic was striking. The interim months have been a difficult time for everyone across the globe and our decision to add a little more uncertainty into our lives by writing our first book at the same time, added to the mix.

Our grateful thanks go to our **lovely partners Liz and Stephen** and our **brilliant families and friends** for their support during this exciting and challenging time. We couldn't have done this without them.

Thanks also go to our **fabulous early readers** who have been kind enough to take time out of their busy days, read chapters of our book and give their thoughts, ideas, and constructive feedback. Thank you one and all!

We wanted to make our business book less formal and **Simon from Scartoons (www.scartoons.co.uk)** has done a great job in providing his unique illustrations to lighten the read. Respect!

Thanks also to **Kirsty at Peacock Digital Marketing (www.peacockdigitalmarketing.co.uk)** for branding our business plan documents. Great job!

INTRODUCTION

Start a Small UK Business.

Business Planning Tools to turn your Ideas into Business Success.

So, you have a great idea for a new business, and you are confident that you can make money out of your proposed product or innovative service.

But can you?

That is the key question!

Starting up a new business can be an extremely rewarding experience, but for those who are new to entrepreneurship, it can be a challenging time.

If you are up for the challenge, we have developed 16 **simple, focused and highly effective** business planning tools, to aid you in 'testing' your target market and considering a number of financial aspects.

Covering many elements of starting up a new business, these interactive documents will allow you to:

Research your **Target Customers**
Analyse your **Competitors**
Develop a **Marketing—Sales and Customer Service** Strategy
Calculate your **Personal Survival Budget** (how much you will need to earn to cover your **personal living expenses**)
Prepare first-time **Business Cashflow** forecasts
Consider your **Personal Skills development** requirements, including **Confidence levels** and **Organisational ability**.
And much more…

Packed with useful hints, tips and tactics and written in an easy to understand, informal style, it will be your essential guide to developing your Business Plan.

Starting up a new business without a business plan is like driving from Land's End to John O'Groats without a road map or satnav. Imagine starting that challenging journey with no idea which way to go or how to get there! Do you travel alone, or will you need someone else onboard to share the driving?

What if you run into heavy traffic on the way and have no contingency plan to help you get back on track, or divert around roadblocks? How do you know how much fuel you will need for the journey? Could you potentially run out of money en route?

Our business plan outlines the 5 'drivers' which we believe are absolutely key to consider when starting up a new business, to ensure that your journey is a successful one. It also includes all the necessary business planning worksheets and documentation (16-available to download).

We have also included several helpful links which will develop your knowledge further as you become more confident and experienced, so as to not overwhelm you as you start up.

Specially written for business start-up sole traders with little or no experience and not vat registered, this book will give you a

robust framework to develop your new business idea and get it up and running successfully.

The information is relevant to anyone who is considering becoming self-employed with much of the best practice guidance valid for all businesses.

We have developed these business planning documents, worksheets and best practice ideas after many years of working with start-up business owners. We are extremely excited to introduce them to you.

We believe that our book is different as we are writing for a new generation of entrepreneurs!

CHAPTER 1

BRAND YOU! DEVELOPING YOUR BRAND

> **Bluebell Worksheet to download for this chapter:**
> **'Brand You' Worksheet**

You are seriously thinking about starting up a new business and the thought is going round and round in your mind. It may be that you are wanting the flexibility of working for yourself, you may have recently been made redundant, or you might have a great product idea that you believe will make you money. You need to do a little research and make a few plans and then you will be away. That is brilliant and very exciting…

but

Before you make that momentous decision to actually start up a new business, you need to work through your thoughts and proposals in a business plan which will ensure that you have considered all the key elements that will help your proposed business to have the greatest chance of success.

That is what we aim to provide you with, and by working through the business plan documents and worksheets available to download, you will have all the information that you need to ensure you get off to the very best start.

In addition, whilst you are working on the details of your proposed business you will also need to take a close look at yourself as the business owner. This is a really great opportunity to consider your skills and look at how your business can utilise and help you build on them. It's also good to understand any areas where you have knowledge gaps. This is important as you will be an integral part of the business as the face of the brand and therefore, critical to its success. It is helpful to understand your strengths and any areas where you need more knowledge as you move forward to building business plans. We will cover this subject in more detail later and give you lots of support throughout, but at this point we just want you to be aware of this aspect while you are starting to compile your plans.

Please, don't be afraid of this. You will work through a document that collects your thoughts on your strengths and any areas where you feel you could be stronger. It also asks you to think of the new opportunities which will open up for you when you become an entrepreneur and any areas in which you have concerns. Having worked through this exercise you will be able to understand the links between you, and your new business, much better. This will be a great help as you go forward.

This will come later in Chapter 5 (Personal Character & Skills Analysis) but for now, we want you to be clear about the link between you and your brand:

Brand You. Your brand!

Our planning documents will take you through this important subject in a simple and readily understandable way. These will lead you through the key aspects and help you understand:

- Why do you want to go into business? E.g., new beginning, improved lifestyle.
- What experience (if any) do you have to support a new business?
- What skills can you bring to the business which will make the journey easier?
- What skills do you need to learn? E.g., Do you lack organisational skills both personal and business (as the two are inextricably linked)?
- Are your finances strong to get you through the first few months or perhaps you have had money problems in the past and your financial track record isn't the best?
- How much money do you need to earn from the business to cover your personal living expenses? You will need to produce this level of income as a minimum, so it is important to know what this figure is before you start.
- Do you have confidence that you have got 'what it takes' or do you have low self-esteem or a lack of self-belief?

We can help you to fully consider these aspects as well as determining your motivations for becoming an entrepreneur. We have worked with many start-up businesspeople, and we aim to ensure that you have a clear understanding of what development areas you may have so that you can be forearmed on setting up your business.

We will concentrate on ensuring that you are confident regarding your organisational skills, both personal and business, as we find that this is an area that most new entrepreneurs need help with. We also find that lack of confidence, even in people who have had successful careers previously, can be a de-motivator when they are moving into a new field with their proposed business. This is called 'Imposter

Syndrome' and there are many good books on the subject if you would like to delve further:

We would recommend Dr Emee Vida Estacio's best seller:

<u>Imposter Syndrome Remedy</u>

VERY IMPORTANT INFORMATION REGARDING ACCESSING THE DOCUMENT AND LINKS LIBRARY

Before we start to understand what elements make up the face of the 'Brand You' that you will show to the **world we need to advise where you can find our document and links libraries.**
To add to your reading experience, here and throughout the book, we have supplied a number of hyperlinks. These are relevant to each chapter and will allow you to delve deeper into the subject matter. **The link library is held on our website (to ensure that we can keep it up to date) and clicking on any blue highlighted link in the book will take you directly there if you are reading the Kindle version. Alternatively, if you are reading the paperback book, go to the address bar at the top of your browser window and enter the following link: https://startupbusinessplanning.co.uk/start-a-small-uk-business-download-and-links.**
These links provide information from the UK Government and others which will be invaluable when you are setting up your business.

In addition, we have developed a document library. Each document is specially and carefully designed so that you can capture the learning points and your thoughts and ideas from each chapter. Then, by the end of the book you will have a full, robust start-up plan for your new business. All you will have to do is 'polish' it!
**You can access these documents from the box at the start of each chapter for the e-book. Click on the document you require, and you will be taken to the document library where you can download a Microsoft Word, Excel or PDF document.
For the paperback, as above, go to: https://startupbusinessplanning.co.uk/start-a-small-uk-business-download-and-links.
The password you will need to access these links and documents on our website is Blu3b3!!**

What will 'Brand You' Look Like?

Once you can better understand your reasons for starting up your business and the fundamentals you will need to work through to improve your chance of success, you will need to consider what your brand will look like. How do you want to represent yourself? Have a look at the following points and begin to visualise your brand.

✓ **Business Name**

As a sole trader, your business name choice is a major decision. It may be that you want to use your own name in some form, as this can give buyers' confidence that you are happy to link your name to your enterprise. Alternatively, you may prefer to choose something that reflects your business activity. Whichever you decide, there are rules that you need to be aware of. Please see the government website below:

<u>Set Up as a Sole Trader - Gov.UK</u>

✓ **Website Domain Name**

In this age of social media, it is essential to have an online presence to promote your brand. To achieve this, your first option will be a website, which will become your virtual shop window. Even if you have an actual shop, it is still wise to have a supporting online option too. Think coronavirus and lockdown. This could be the saving grace for your business!

The first step is for you to purchase a domain name.

This is the unique online address where internet users can access your website. There are several providers of domain names on the internet, and we would recommend that you do an internet search and compare prices and service options before you decide upon who to use. These sites give you guidance on selecting an appropriate domain name. You will need to renew your domain name each year for as long as your website is active.

You can choose a domain name that matches your business name or that has a link to your product or service e.g., our business is called Bluebell Business, but our website domain name is startupbusiness-planning.co.uk. You will need to consider what potential customers will be searching for when you make your final decision.

The domain name extension, in our case .co.uk, shows that we are based in the UK. You could alternatively choose one linked to your business activities e.g., .biz .net.

(To understand how to optimise your web site, see Chapter 4 where we give more information).

You can see that whatever you choose will need to fully reflect your brand.

✓ Logo

This is a unique symbol that represents your business, and you will use it on your business cards, website, social media, etc. It will encapsulate your brand both in design and colour. Think of well-known brand logos like the McDonalds red and yellow M.

There are websites where you can design a logo yourself for a small fee or you can employ a graphic designer to create a logo for you to reflect your brand. Of course, this will cost more, and you will need to ensure that you obtain the rights to use the logo for your business from the designer. Some designers include this in the purchase price, but it is best to make sure!

✓ Strap Line

This is a sentence that encapsulates the philosophy of your brand.

Short and sweet! It is usually included where your logo is shown. Some well-known examples:

I'm lovin' it—McDonalds.
Every little helps—Tesco.
Because you're worth it—L'Oreal.

It is important that your logo and strap line are unique as many companies trademark theirs and these cannot be copied.

What will yours be?

✓ Colours

The colour or colours that you choose to show your brand personality will have a meaning for prospective customers. The psychology of colour has been studied and colour plays a greater role in influencing our purchases than we might think!

Here we show some of the main colours that marketers have studied and the emotions they create.

> **Red:** Excitement and Passion/High in energy, sense of urgency.
> **Blue:** Peace and reliability/Calming and provides a sense of security and trust in brands.
> **Green:** Health, Tranquillity, and nature/Reliability brands
> **Purple:** Royalty, wisdom, and respect/creative, wise, and imaginative brands.
> **Orange and Yellow:** Cheerfulness, optimism and enthusiasm/draws in impulsive buyers and window shoppers.
> **Black:** Sophistication, class and power/Used by luxury brands.
> **White:** Cleanliness, minimalistic and purity/Minimalistic and functional brands.

✓ Consistency

Once you have decided on what your brand will look like, including your logo, strapline, colours, and fonts, it is particularly important to be consistent across all areas where you interact with customers e.g., website, business cards, marketing materials, leaflets etc. **This is essential**. Imagine reading a leaflet and being really interested in the product advertised, going to the website with the aim of ordering but being confused because the website has a completely different look and colour to the leaflet. Any customer uncertainty can lose you a sale! Ensure that your brand is always clearly represented.

✓ Work Wear

Depending upon the type of business that you are going to be running, it is important to consider what will be suitable to wear in your new role. What image do you want to portray whilst representing your business? If your business is to be a traditional one, you may want to be formally dressed. If it is a modern, fun one you may prefer to wear smart, casual clothes. For those starting up in a tradesperson role, a smart T-shirt with an embroidered logo would be suitable, in brand colours of course!

Once you start to employ staff, they are representing your brand and so name badges with your logo and brand colours for workwear are appropriate.

Whatever you decide, be consistent, reflect your brand.

✓ Values

It is essential to consider the core values by which you intend to run your business and interact with your customers. They may be personal to you e.g., to be customer focused, or they may be linked to social values like improving the environment by sourcing items sustainably, for example. Your customers will want to hear about your values, and if they share your views they may be more likely to buy from you, it is, therefore, important to publish them.

✓ Mission Statement

Once you are clear as to the values you want your business to reflect in your day-to-day dealings, it will help you to clarify how you will use those values by writing a mission statement. A mission statement articulates purpose; it explains what your business does, expressed in a way that encapsulates the values that are important to you.

First explain what your business does e.g., provide pet walking service, manufacture cosmetics, sell baby paraphernalia, design phone apps. Then explain how you wish to do business and what values are important to you.

Let's take the cosmetics manufacturer as an example. She intends to hand blend cosmetics at her home. The cosmetics will be plant-based, vegan, and cruelty-free. No synthetics or chemicals will be used. She wants to provide high-quality products supported by a high standard of customer service.

The products will be packaged in glass and fully recyclable containers to help the environment via customers' recycling and re-using.

Her mission statement might read like this:

> "We are an artisan cosmetics company. We hand make plant-based, vegan cosmetics, which are good for you and your skin as they do not contain synthetics or chemicals, just caring, nourishing ingredients. We use glass and fully recyclable plastic containers to hold our products and our postal packaging is recyclable, reusable, and biodegradable. In this way, we aim to protect our environment by allowing customers to recycle and re-use our containers and packaging. We couple this with high levels of customer service, and we intend to donate £1 per product sold to the charity Plastic Oceans UK."

In small businesses, the owner is the brand and should live and reflect his or her brand values. This will ensure that customers will become fans of the brand seeing a consistent approach from the brand leader.

You now have lots of information to help you to create your brand and its look and 'feel'. A few words of advice from us: please stay true to yourself whilst working through this process. You will find it much easier to maintain your brand values via customer interactions if you genuinely believe in what you have created.

This is the start of your business planning journey, and we have prepared a

<u>Bluebell 'Brand You' Worksheet</u>

to capture your brand ideas whilst they are fresh in your mind. Please click on the link at the start of the chapter to download the document and enjoy getting your thoughts down on paper. In the next chapter, we will look at business planning in more detail and you will be able to start to build your plan.

Before we move on let's think back to the road map analogy we mentioned in the book description and the journey you are on:

Starting up a new business without a business plan is like driving from Land's End to John O'Groats without a road map or satnav. Imagine starting that challenging journey with no idea which way to go or how to get there! Do you travel alone, or will you need someone else onboard to share the driving?

What if you run into heavy traffic on the way and have no contingency plan to help you get back on track, or divert around roadblocks? How do you know how much fuel you will need for the journey? Could you potentially run out of money en route?

'Brand You' is the vehicle you are driving. Is it a bright coloured, top of the range, fast, luxury brand or is it a mid-range vehicle, steady and reliable, or a budget run about town car? You will need to be clear about what image you are projecting as your branding will be the first thing your prospective customers see, and it will need to reflect you and your business!

CHAPTER 2

BUSINESS PLANNING—CREATING YOUR PLAN

Key Driver

> **Bluebell documents to download for this chapter:**
> **Business Plan Summary**
> **Jotter**

For all new entrepreneurs, the production of a business plan is the single most important exercise to undertake before starting up in business. We have explained why you need a 'road map' for your business in the introduction and we reiterate that here. Working through your business plan will allow you to ensure, that what we believe are the 5 key drivers to business success, are inherent in your business planning and will give you the best chance to get your new business up and running successfully. So, let's get that plan underway.

First, we need to tackle those ideas running around in your head!

From the moment that you have a great idea for your new business, it is essential to grab a notebook and pen, your phone notepad, or dictation facility, to jot down all your thoughts as they appear to you. You will find that they rush around your head at such a speed that if you fail to write them down straight away, whether night or day, you will be unable to recall the detail later and that is so frustrating!

At this stage do not try to analyse or validate your ideas, just write **everything** down for later consideration. Do not cross anything out! It is helpful to put a date against each entry so that you know how long the item has been outstanding! What you are effectively doing, unconsciously, is brainstorming.

Some of you might prefer to use our Bluebell Business Jotter. A one-page document that you can download from our website, it is designed to help you capture your thoughts and manage the process of transferring your notes to your formal business plan in a streamlined way.

Bluebell Jotter Extract

Due Date	Priority	Business Plan Action Point Detail	Status	Added to Business Plan/Worksheet
Example	High	Market Research - Mystery Shop Main Competitor	Completed	Yes
Example	Low	Brand You - Strap Line Ideas	Pending	
Example	Medium	Personal Survival Budget - Get Bank Statements	In progress	

Bluebell Business — Enabling Business Growth

Bluebell Business Jotter FOR [enter name]

> **Bluebell Tip**
>
> We have found that this exercise of writing every idea down is beneficial in helping to clear your mind, providing space for new ideas to form, and ensuring that you capture the detail of all your thoughts for later analysis.

In a short time, your notebook, or jotter, will have lots of ideas in note form to work on and if you are to move your proposed business forward, it is important to deal with these notes in an organised way.

- So, what is the best way to do that? Well, the aim is for you to go through each of your notes, research and validate them and consider which items should make it onto your 'official' business plan. **You are looking for those items which show promise and are likely to add value and make your business a success.**
- You may find it helpful, once you start to work on your business plan, to find space in a quiet 'corner' of your home where you can look at your notes in detail whenever you have an opportunity. It will also help if you can block time out of your diary, so you have a structured approach to getting your business plan researched and written.
- If you are working while you are developing your business this approach is even more essential! You may find that you are more productive first thing in the morning, so putting a diary slot into your morning schedule to work on your business plan will move your plan forward very successfully. However, if you are a night owl, a diary slot in the evening might suit you better. Whatever you chose, it will become part of your routine, and a habit, in a very short time.
- You will find it beneficial to categorise and order your notes e.g., market research notes are grouped together, as it is much more productive to deal with them in this way. As you work through them, you will naturally prioritise them, as it will

become obvious that some should be actioned or researched before others and so you will need to start on these first. You may also find it helpful to give notes in each category an A, B or C rating to indicate priority (A being high, B medium, and C low) which will help you to quickly see which note to start on next.

- Once you have completed your research, put a line through (or strike out) the note but leave it visible as you will need to transfer any relevant detail to your worksheets/final business plan to confirm that you have fully considered this aspect. Essentially what you are doing is using the note pad/jotter as your 'draft plan'.
- At this stage you will have many ideas that will not make the 'final cut' but using the note pad/jotter in this way will make you more organised as the ideas flood in.
- Every 7 days or so, go back and look at previous notes. Any left unactioned or unfinished, carry forward to the latest page. This will ensure that you action or research every idea that has come into your mind, and none will be forgotten.

Whilst you are working your way through your notes and as you confirm (or otherwise) your thoughts and assumptions regarding your new business, this is the time to start to transfer your information across to our worksheets. These worksheets are designed to link to each chapter and will form the basis of your business plan.

So, the process is:

---

1. Capture all your thoughts in your notebook or jotter. Those that are running through your mind, together with those ideas which are generated as you go through each chapter.

---

2. Research/validate each note and clearly mark those which are to be included in your final business plan.

---

3. Transfer all your validated notes onto the appropriate worksheets. These worksheets will form the basis of your business plan.

They are downloadable from the links at the top of each chapter (for Kindle readers) or from our website http://www.startupbusinessplanning.co.uk (for paperback readers).

We recommend that you download them to a computer rather than an e-book reader.

---

4. Finally, you will complete your business plan with the Bluebell Business Plan summary sheet which is downloadable from the link at the start of this chapter.

This will provide an overview of your research and the conclusions that you have drawn from working through your plan.

Your Business Plan will then contain:

Business Plan Summary Sheet
'Brand You' Worksheet
Market and Competitor Research Worksheet
Avatar Planners
Marketing-Sales and Customer Service Worksheet
Personal Character & Skills Analysis & Action Plan
Personal Survival Budget
Cashflow Forecast

This may seem like a challenging task, but we aim to take you through each of these stages of your planning journey, providing hints, tips tactics and best practice, to enable you to write a successful plan.

Let's recap: Every business needs a business plan (remember it is your map to a successful business journey). We ask you to make notes initially so that you can explore your journey on paper and work through potential scenarios, check your figures and marketplace and reassure yourself that you have a viable (profitable) idea before you actually start up your business. It should give you great confidence that you are doing the right thing.

It is good to remember that others may also wish to look at your plan e.g., your bank may be called upon to assist with finances or you may wish to apply for a start-up grant. In both cases, your plan would be perused by others, and this is where new entrepreneurs often write their plan in too formal a way, and it becomes 'a duty' or a 'task that must be done'. This is 'writing for writings sake', where the entrepreneur writes 'reams' but fails to include the key elements that will confirm that the potential business is likely to be successful. After all, that is why the plan is being written! Whereas a business plan which captures the personal excitement of planning for a new venture and the reasons why it is important to you, makes all the difference to the impact of the plan on yourself and others as your voice and personality will come through.

For example, a client of ours had aimed to write a 'professional' business plan and there is nothing wrong with that! She had included pages and pages of information because she honestly believed that was what was needed. Unfortunately, the end result was that it was not interesting as it was too 'wordy' and most of the information was not relevant—it didn't cover the aspects that would show she had a real chance of success, nor did it have 'heart'. In other words, anyone reading the plan would not have their emotions stirred and their interest piqued.

This client was an animal photographer, and her photographs were beautiful. Amazing, unusual shots of animals of all sorts but they were not shown or included in the plan at all, just referred to. The actual sight of these photos had the power to lift the plan out of the ordinary! This was her unique product and it needed to be front and centre of her plan.

Neither had she mentioned that photography had been her hobby since she was a little girl, so she was very experienced and had won awards. Once she had realised that these were particularly important and added credibility to her business aspirations by showing her personal skills and confidence, the whole plan came alive.

The point that we are making is that **this is your plan**, your opportunity to test your ideas and thoughts on paper before taking the important step of starting your new business. It is written by you, for you, but it does not hurt to make it interesting and informative for any other stakeholder or supporter who may become involved in your business. Remember, that these are people you will want to get on your side and 'buy into' the plans you are presenting to them. Please don't get overly concerned with your personal writing style, just make sure that you concentrate on including the 5 key aspects that we are covering in these chapters.

Our keywords are simple, focused, and effective and that is what your business plan should be.

> ### Bluebell Tip
>
> We would also emphasise that this is not a one-off process. All good business owners are regularly planning forward so that when 'curve balls' come along they are better able to cope. We recommend that you review your business plan at least once a year, but you will find as you become more familiar with the process that you will start to update it as you go along.
>
> We will introduce our 'Improvement Circle' to you in Chapter 8. This is a simple method of enabling you to continually review and improve your business plans.

So, let's summarise as there is a lot to take in! Mind racing with ideas:

1. Get them down on paper or add them to your phone notepad. Don't analyse your ideas at this stage just write every one down, including those that come into your mind whilst you are reading through the book.
2. Fully analyse and research each note you have made and identify those that you think will add value to your business.

3. As you go through the book, download the documents/worksheets available for each chapter and transfer any validated notes relevant to that section across from your notepad. You will see your business plan start to take shape as you so this. Remember to make the content interesting and relevant.
4. The Summary for your business plan is available to download at the start of this chapter. You can transfer your validated notes across to the relevant business plan sections. Or you may prefer, where you have completed a worksheet for a particular section, to add the worksheet and make a note to that effect in the relevant section in the summary plan.
5. Don't be afraid to mention in your business plan any ideas that you have eventually decided do not add value but where you want to show that other options have been considered and rejected.

The benefits of approaching your plan in this way are:

- Your thoughts and ideas are never forgotten (what may not work now, may be a helpful pointer in the future).
- All ideas and thoughts will be fully researched.
- You are working on your business planning in 'manageable chunks' so you will not be overwhelmed.
- You will have a fully researched business plan with 'back papers' which can be referred to.
- You will not be writing a business plan as though you are writing an essay or writing "for writings sake," as a number of start-up business owners do, because they are not experienced.
- You will be amazed at how quickly your plan comes together and you will enjoy writing it.
- Once you have confirmed your business is likely to be viable, your confidence will be massively enhanced.
- By approaching your plan in this way, you will be invigorated, and the freeing up of mental space to create order and

allow you to be creative will make you feel great and positive about your business journey.

Before we move forward to our next chapter we would like you to think about your business plan itself and what it must contain. Your plan needs to have very strong foundations and the subjects which are coming up in the next few chapters are those which will help build those foundations for you.

We call these elements the 5 key drivers:

1. **Business Planning** – The overarching discipline of understanding your business, planning well, and using the practice of continuous improvement.
2. **Market Research** – Finding your target market for your product or service. This will improve your sales to customer ratio.
3. **Marketing: Sales & Customer Service** – Employing great sales and service tactics to engage your customers and make them fans who will remain with you, repurchase from you, and recommend you to friends and family.
4. **Personal Character & Skills Analysis** – Understanding your own skills and areas where you are not so strong so as to produce a development plan where you can continually improve as the business owner.
5. **Cashflow Forecasting** – Knowledge of your business and its financial position via regular review and analysis of cash flow forecasts

The stronger the foundations, the more successful your business will be. It will be the difference between you building your business on sand or achieving a strong foundation that will carry your business forward into the future. We will provide lots of tips, hints, tools, and tactics to ensure that you build these strong foundations which will keep your business stable and successful.

Going back to our road map analogy, the business plan is the map itself. It will ensure that you have thoroughly researched all aspects of your journey, worked out the best route to travel, and ensured that you have contingency plans in place if you hit any 'roadblocks' along the way. It will give you the very best chance of getting to your destination i.e., developing a successful business for the future!

We are now going to consider how you find your customers…

CHAPTER 3

MARKET & COMPETITOR RESEARCH—FINDING YOUR CUSTOMERS!

Key Driver

> **Bluebell Documents to download for this chapter:**
> **Market and Competitor Research Worksheet**
> **Avatar Worksheet**

Having thought about your brand, your next step when you are considering setting up a new business is to research and learn about your target audience.

So, what is a target audience?

It is the sector of the population who are most likely to be interested in your product or service and, therefore, the group to which your marketing activities should be aimed.

This sector may be a group of people of a similar age e.g., children, or it might be a group of people of different ages but similar hobbies like gaming, fishing, for instance. They may be at different stages in their lives: teens, college students, new parents, or retirees. Each of these groups will have different characteristics and it is your first task to understand what those traits are. The clearer you can define your target group the better. This is known as segmentation.

> **Bluebell Tip**
>
> Consider your target audience:
> Age? What stage of life?
> Married? Children?
> Disposable Income?
> Where do they live?
> Lifestyle including hobbies?
> What transport do they use?
> What car do they have?
> Work and qualifications?
> What magazines do they read?
> What social media channels do they use?
> What can you offer them to make their life better?
> What can you offer them to provide a solution to a problem they have?

Going through this process, you will start to visualise your target audience and understand who they are, where their interests lie, and home in on where best to spend your marketing budget. **Each group will have its own profile (known as an avatar). It may be that you will have 2 or 3 different customer profiles which seem a good fit for your offering. Once created, concentrate on these key groups.**

A scattergun approach to targeting your customers is unlikely to work and will only dissipate your efforts.

A good tip is to give each Avatar a 'name'. When writing this book, we were researching our target market and came up with our three key target groups:

1. **Part-time Planners**: potential customers who are looking for part-time work and have decided to set up a new business to facilitate this.
2. **Redundant Workers**: potential customers who have been made redundant, maybe because of the Covid-19 crisis? Setting up a new business would be beneficial for them.
3. **Interested Innovators**: potential customers who are innovative and will have new products or technology ideas to sell but may not have a business background to enable them to achieve this.

So, you will see that the issue for all three groups is that they have little or no experience running their own business and how to set it up.

Going through this process, you can start to visualise your key customer groups and can capture the customer avatar description your mind.

To assist in this research, please download our avatar worksheet from the link at the beginning of this chapter. It will assist you in gathering thoughts and ideas to fully develop and personalise your avatars.

Leading marketers are now looking at avatar research in new and interesting ways. They suggest that you look at a before and after situation for the group you have in mind. First, think about the group you have chosen and what their 'pain point' is. The 'pain point' will be the problem for which your product or service will provide a solution. Then consider what their lives will be like having purchased your product.

You will see then, that gaining a full understanding of your target audience is at the heart of your proposed new business and key for any business owner!

It is crucial that you fully understand who your customers are going to be and what they really need from your business. Many entrepreneurs will have an opinion and a view about who their customers are and what they want. This is a great start, but it is important to rigorously confirm your assumptions are correct. Once you have defined them, you should review them regularly.

Here are steps to identify your target customers:

---

1. Create a customer profile, also known as an avatar. An avatar is a great tool for understanding your prospective customer group. It is a composite description of the people who are most likely to buy your products or services. They will share certain characteristics and creating an avatar will help you to visualise that person and their lifestyle choices clearly.

Your <u>avatar worksheet</u> will help you consider all aspects of key customer profiles so that you can understand who they are and where to find them.

---

2. You can learn about your target audience through effective market research.

---

3. Once you have your first avatar profile written down, go out and meet these individuals or businesses. Talk to them, listen to them, and learn all you can.

---

4. Remember, during discussions, to look out for patterns in their feedback of any needs, desires or demands they have relating to your product or service.

---

5. Dovetail this information into your business offering where appropriate.

---

6. Tailor your website and social media accounts to share and take advantage of this information.

---

7. Of course, your proposed customers may be other businesses rather than individual consumers, but this process is still valid.

This is the fun part!

Getting 'close and personal' with your potential customers, talking to them about your business idea and gaining their (hopefully) constructive feedback about your product or service is a very productive activity for all new start-up business owners.

(For those of you who feel they might struggle with this aspect of developing your business, please don't worry. We cover a lack of confidence in Chapter 5).

Yes, of course, you will have spoken to your family and friends, and whilst their comments will be helpful and supportive, they are less likely to tell you any negative thoughts that they have. Therefore, it is so important to get feedback from your target audience—those people who are potential customers and may want to buy from you.

Bluebell Tip

Having once defined their target audience, businesses that become successful take an additional important step. They check to see if their assumptions and opinions are correct by talking to their potential customers.

This can be achieved in a few ways:

- on a 'one-to-one' basis
- organising a survey on an appropriate social media platform e.g., Facebook, Instagram LinkedIn etc., or via MailChimp.
- Getting a group of potential customers together in a customer forum. This could be online e.g., Zoom, Teams or 'face to face' (socially distant where appropriate).
- It is of the utmost importance to listen to the feedback given by your prospective customers.

Your target audience research should be based on the feedback that comes from your potential customers and not your personal assumptions!

You will find that this additional research will give you so much more information about your customers and their needs, so that you can design your offering and related services to match and thereby, make your business more successful.

You must regularly refresh your research via customer surveys, feedback, and online reviews as fashions and opinions change.

So why is finding this target group so important?

If you're going fishing you need to know what fish you are trying to catch, and what bait to use on the hook.

If you don't go fishing you don't catch fish!

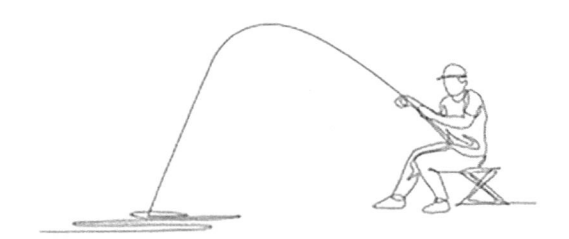

Think of this: Watch 'Morse' on ITV 3 on a weekday morning and look at the adverts shown in the breaks. For those of you who don't know, Morse is a detective chief inspector working on murder cases in Oxford in the 1980s and 1990s. The businesses who advertise when this programme is on know their target audience extremely well and will have categorised them. They are likely to be aged 55+, retired and when watching Morse will have a feeling of nostalgia. So, for that target group, the adverts shown relate to funeral plans, life cover, stairlifts, self-lifting chairs, and mobility scooters.

There would be no point in showing these adverts when a programme designed for a younger age group is showing. A good example would be the programme 'Love Island' because the target audience demographics are quite different. Love island is a programme where 10 singles stay at a villa for a few weeks and have to couple up with each other. Whilst this programme is showing, adverts are young fashion brands which suit an 18-30 target audience.

This clearly illustrates the importance of the correct 'bait' for your target audience to ensure sales success.

> ### Bluebell Tip
>
> Simply put, it would not be cost-effective to pay for a young fashion advert during the Morse program.
> No sales would be achieved!
> Nor would a stairlift advert be successful while Love Island is being shown!

So, we are clear that talking to your target audience is especially important and you will be keen to get onto that, but you may be unsure how to go about it.

Initially, the internet is the best starting resource for your research, but please don't ignore other avenues such as libraries, telephone, and trade directories. Local Chambers of Commerce are an excellent resource too! This type of research is unsurprisingly called **Desk Research.**

Let's imagine that you are setting up a business related to fishing. People of all ages are interested in that so a search on Google, Facebook, or Instagram (amongst others) will bring up several fishing clubs and societies in your local area. A phone call or message to 2 or 3 of the clubs will allow you to arrange subsequent visits to speak to members. This will provide an amazing amount of market feedback direct from your target audience. This is known as **Field Research** and is the primary method of learning about your target customers. This is because you are getting the information direct from people who are customer prospects. The benefits of doing this cannot be underestimated.

We have met new business owners who have started up having never spoken directly to a prospective customer. This is a mistake, but an easy one to make when you are inexperienced! As we said earlier, it is important to confirm that your assumptions are correct, and you cannot do this without speaking directly to your target audience.

Bluebell Tip

When preparing for a customer forum, create a list of questions as it is easy for your mind to go blank, especially if you are face to face with potential customers.

Ask good open questions which start with one of the following: How, Why, Which, Who, When, What, as you will get more than just yes or no answers e.g.

- How do you think I can improve my product?
- What more could I offer?

If you want to confirm your understanding—closed questions are best as you will get a clear yes or no answer e.g.

- Have I missed anything?
- Is that correct?

TED questions are good too as you can obtain more detailed information. TED is a mnemonic, which means that each letter is the first letter of a word. This is a memory aid! So, in this example, the letters for TED mean **Tell, Explain** & **Describe.**

- Perhaps you could **tell** me why you prefer that design?
- Could you **explain** why that would be of more benefit to you?
- Please **describe** the levels of service that you would expect from me.

> It is also best practice to have some **'pre-start-up' business cards** made up when doing field research. At this stage, you might not have fully decided on a name for your proposed business, nor a logo or branding, however, it is essential that you can leave your contact details with your prospective customers and obtain theirs in return (remembering to get permission to contact them). If your business does go ahead you will have a pre-prepared contact list available, and they will be able to get in contact with you. Win-Win!
>
> It is also worth noting that there are virtual business cards and apps becoming available, allowing you to share your contact details via phone. This is eco friendly and companies such as Popl provide a digital card or visit your app store for phone based ones.

It is extremely useful to have a pre-prepared ideas tick list for your target customers to choose from, but please do not close your mind to other ideas that come out of the discussions. These are often the best!

You will then need to analyse the results, take note of any patterns which emerge (such as any needs, desires, demands, or comments that your prospects make—especially if these are mentioned by more than one person), and apply common sense to how you can make best use of the feedback by integrating appropriate ideas into your business processes.

At this point, you may be asking how this research will help to make your business more successful?

A client of ours was considering setting up a dog walking business.

He undertook some desk research and identified two potential target groups to investigate further.

Target Group	**Target Group**
 Working individuals/couples with disposable income and a dog.	 Elderly/frail retired Individuals/Couples with disposable income and a dog.
Pain Point: Worry that their dog is unable to be let out during the day. 	**Pain Point:** Concern that they are unable to give their dog a good walk. 
Avatar: Turn Worried Workers into Reassured Owners. 	**Avatar:** Turn Concerned Retirees into Contented Owners. 

His challenge was how to find them.

This was his desk research:

He first needed to find people with dogs so started by doing an internet search on local pet stores/supermarkets, their addresses and contact numbers. He then found a local dog training group's meeting venue and contact number, and finally, he obtained details of a couple of local vets.

He then decided to create a simple questionnaire which he would use to test the validity of his dog walking idea and confirm his customer groups. He had twelve questions that he would have liked to ask potential customers but realised that wouldn't be appropriate to ask them all on one questionnaire. He, therefore, split the questions across two questionnaires and planned to alternate them in his discussions. The final question on each was "If I set up this dog walking business would you be a potential customer?"

He first spoke to the two pet stores in his local area. He asked for permission to approach their customers and was allowed to proceed. He chose the questions he would ask with great care, and he intended to ask each individual or family group no more than six.

He next contacted the dog training group and arranged a time to visit so that he could chat with dog owners at the start and end of their sessions. He intended to hand out his two questionnaires and go back the following week to pick them up.

Finally, he approached both vets and obtained permission to sit in their waiting rooms and speak to dog owners and leave questionnaires. He knew he would need to be sensitive when choosing who to speak to.

His field research:

He followed up on all his plans, attending the pet stores, dog training group and vets. He was able to approach people who appeared to be in his target groups and was able to confirm some of his assumptions e.g., that prospective customers would expect him to carry appropriate insurance. But he was surprised at some of the questions he was asked, and he was able to add several customer suggestions/needs into his proposed business model.

Following target market field research discussions with forty people, twenty-three expressed a wish for some basic behavioural training for their dogs during walks. To gain the business of these twenty-three potential customers, it made common sense for him to include this training in his service offering. Ten others wanted him to have basic first aid training and again, this seemed an advantageous selling point for him. He had to undertake the appropriate training himself first, but it opened the door for a higher price point being accepted by these target groups.

In this example, the dog walker, having taken this suggestion on board, improved his income, improved his service offering and engaged with his new customers. It is also likely that these new customers will recommend him to friends and family.

You can see that if you can correctly profile your target customers, your marketing campaigns will be so much more effective. The danger is that if you don't know who your customers are, how can you effectively target them and test your assumptions?

You cannot sell something to people who are not interested in your product or service. It's that simple!

The more clearly you define your target group the better you can understand how and where to reach your best prospects and achieve the best possible sales conversion rates.

At this stage, it's also a good idea to research your competitors and find out what they offer.

Bluebell Tip

A good way to research your competitors is by 'mystery' shopping. This should be a mixture of face to face (if the competitor has an outlet), by telephone, and online.

You should be looking to see what you can learn from the interactions.

Some Examples:

Are there any great customer service skills in evidence e.g., excellent telephone answering? Many new business owners forget to answer the telephone professionally, neither do they put a business answerphone message on their mobile phones. Many sales can be lost as potential customers are not sure that they are through to the correct person as they get a generic message.

What products and/or services are available?
Is the competitor offering something which you haven't even thought of?
What is their pricing like?
Are they at the basic, standard, or luxury end of the market?

Do they respond to website/social media queries in an acceptable timeframe?
Potential customers like a prompt response or they will go elsewhere.

It is worthwhile to keep the details of your research on your competitors, their products, or services, and regularly update them.

There is nothing more frustrating than losing customers to a competitor because they have introduced a new and relevant service that you were not aware of!

Now you have lots of information about what your target audience really wants, and what your competitors offer, it's time to tailor your product or service to meet their needs.

> **Bluebell Tip**
>
> Remember to **always** stay close to your customers by checking in with their needs as new trends develop and customer demand changes.
>
> By keeping close to your customers, you can often pick up an advantageous selling point for your business. Most business plans expect a unique selling point, but these can be difficult to find! We prefer to look for an advantageous selling point.

A client of ours was setting up a business as an electrician. He had been an employed, professionally qualified electrician for many years but had decided to set up his own business as he wanted more flexibility in his working hours to meet his family's needs. Whilst completing his market research plan, he was struggling to find a unique selling point for his business as most existing electricians offer remarkably similar services. He, therefore, decided to find an advantageous selling point. During his face-to-face customer research, it became clear that it would be to his advantage to consider his service offering. Several of his target audience prospects mentioned the fact that sometimes tradespeople had been inconsiderate when working in their homes. Now he had something to work on, and using the feedback, he developed his service strategy.

One element was that before entering a client's home, he would drop a small rubber-backed mat through the door. The mat had his business name and logo printed on it. He would step onto the mat and put on shoe covers before stepping onto the client's carpet. Clients were so impressed by his consideration that they often recommended him to friends and family. He had created an advantageous selling point that customers liked very much, and he built upon it by carrying a small hand-held vacuum with him to clean his work areas.

If his electrical work had not been up to scratch his service offering wouldn't have been so effective. As it was, he received many referrals and recommendations because of this strategy. This might seem a small offering, but it has had a massively positive impact on his sales.

So, now let us introduce you to:

The Bluebell Market Research Pendulum

So how will you know when you have done enough market research to confirm your initial assumptions? Well, we have developed this tool to give you a full understanding of that!

The image above is a pendulum, and we are going to use this to ask ourselves the key question "How effective is my market research?"

A negative swing to the left indicates extremely poor market research, the middle position indicates 'so, so' market research, and a maximum positive swing to the right indicates exemplary market research.

To give an example of the pendulum swing, we are going to look at the market research of talented artist, Dianne, who is looking to start up her new business:

The aim is to paint (no pun intended here!) three scenarios to illustrate a point using the pendulum.

Scenario 1

"I am an artist who wants to become self-employed, working 3 days a week giving art lessons. I have a real passion for art so I'm going to put a few flyers about, order some business cards, and get the show on the road."

So where does the pendulum sit in terms of effective market research in this scenario?

Well, it's bang over to the left—full on ineffective. The artist in this scenario is basing her business on her own opinion without checking her thoughts with the people who will be buying from her.

In our experience as business advisers, many startup business owners launch straight into trading without any market research and most certainly, increase the chance of early failure.

As we have said earlier, it is those businesses that take that next important step, to check or substantiate their opinion with their target audience, who are the most successful. Why check it out with them? Simple, they will be the ones who will be paying for the service!

Scenario 2

"I am an artist who wants to become self-employed, working 3 days a week giving art lessons. I have a real passion for art so I'm going to put a few flyers about, order some business cards, and get the show on the road. But I'm also going to do a bit of market research as my business adviser told me it was important. So, this is what I did:

I spoke to my family to ask them what they thought. They thought it was a great idea as they'd seen my work and knew how committed I was. I also spoke to my friends to ask them what they thought. They also thought it was a great idea; they too had seen my work, knew how passionate I was and also told me I would make an excellent teacher. I'm now going to put a few flyers about, order some business cards, and get my business started as I've done my market research."

So where does the pendulum sit in terms of effective market research?

Well, it sits over to the left and it's poor. Yes, some market research has been done but not with the target audience, only with family and friends. Again, in our experience, these close contacts very often give great feedback but from an encouragement point of view rather than fact-based.

Scenario 3

"I am an artist who wants to become self-employed, working 3 days a week giving art lessons. The classes will be for beginners. I have a real passion for art so I'm going to get the show on the road.

First things first.

I set about writing my business plan with market research as my start point.

I first needed to understand who my target audience was likely to be, so I started with desktop research and simply made an internet search for art lessons.

From the results, I chose 3 target groups as a starting point, but it was important for me to keep an open mind about this as my field research could well show that these were not the right target groups for my business.

The 3 target groups I selected were:

Retired adults—not working.
Working individuals likely to attend evening classes.
School-age children.

The second thrust of my market research was a mix of desktop research and field research, the majority of which was field research. I wanted it this way because people buy people and my business by its very nature—teaching—is people to people based. I felt I could also read body language more readily with face to face, field research and it allowed me the freedom to improvise and adapt my research with these people and learn more from them.

My first market research was with a local college. I discovered they were having an open day for the next term's evening classes and the college wanted feedback from exhibitors on the day to ascertain the most popular courses to put on. Potential exhibitors were invited to apply, so I applied, and I was able to secure a stand.

The second thrust of my market research was with The University of the Third Age (U3A). I had noticed from my desktop research that U3A ran an annual art competition.

I contacted the local U3A chairperson and asked 2 simple questions: First, did they think there would be a place for my art lessons? The answer to that question was yes. My second question was what would be the best way of reaching that audience?

I was told there definitely was an appetite for art lessons and was invited to give a short presentation at the next 2-day networking event. This would allow me to position my offer and to mingle with the people afterwards, to further develop my market research.

For both days I planned my approach thoroughly.

I had:

- A prepared list of well thought through questions. The questions were a mix of open, closed, and TED questions.
- A free prize draw was offered to participants.
- Examples of my work.
- A " pre-startup" set of business cards with my contact details.
- A notebook to record people's responses and comments to ensure nothing was missed. Then if patterns emerged, I could spot them quickly and delve deeper by adapting my questions.
- My CV.
- I also decided to book a room at the college, so that I could offer a free taster lesson.

I was fully prepared to attend the college open day and the UA3 networking event.

I thoroughly enjoyed both days!

So, what did I learn? How did my market research go?

Both days were extremely productive, and the market research confirmed some of the assumptions I had made, but I was also surprised to learn from my target audience some aspects I had not considered.

To summarise the college market research:

An analysis of responses to my questions suggested there was a market for my art classes. I analysed the number of people I spoke to, against the positive responses I received and concluded that with this target audience, 20% responded positively with real interest and three booked onto the free taster session.

Other things I learned that I had not considered, were that I needed to choose appropriate lesson start and finish times that would work in line with family commitments and school runs.

A pattern also emerged from customer responses. 63% thought it would be a good idea to include a 20-minute coffee break during the lesson to allow people to get to know each other and share thoughts and ideas about their artwork. This was something I had not considered!

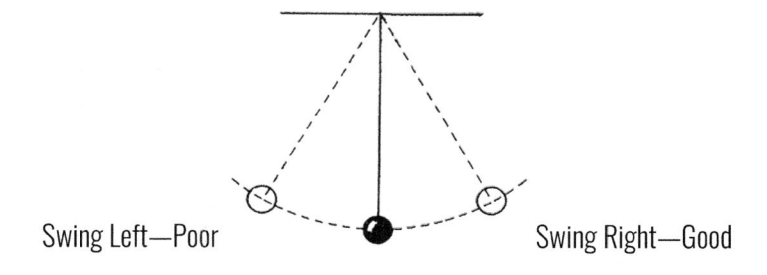

Swing Left—Poor   Swing Right—Good

Question:
How would you mark Dianne's scenario 3 market research so far?

To summarise my UA3 Market research:

The presentation I made at the two-day networking event was well received with a surprising number of questions. I concluded the presentation by saying I was staying behind for the networking and I would be available to talk more.

Again, an analysis of responses to my questions suggested there was a market for my art classes but in this target group, the responses were more positive. I analysed the number of people I spoke to against the positive responses I received and concluded with this target audience that 43%

responded positively with real interest and six bookings onto the free taster session at the college.

I ran my free taster course being mindful of the suggested start and finish times from my market research.

From my market research, I ensured I included a coffee break with ample time to allow effective networking.

I was really pleased as all nine attended and the lesson went well with all nine booking onto and paying for my initial three-month 'Art for Beginners' lesson programme.

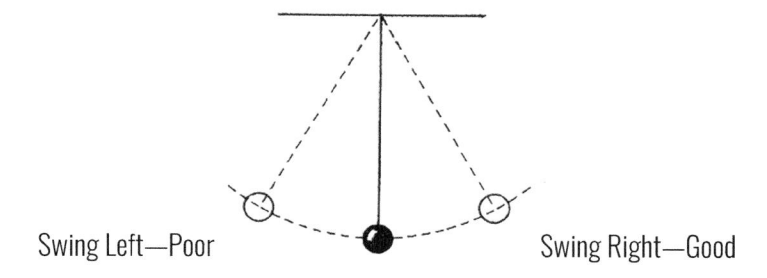

Swing Left—Poor   Swing Right—Good

How would you mark her scenario 3 market research now?

I was extremely pleased with my initial market research findings and felt this was a great starting point for my goal of working three days a week. I think I'd better update my Marketing Research and Sales Plan and put a note in my diary to renew my market research in six months!

What can we learn from our artist entrepreneur?

Scenario 1 – It is not appropriate when undertaking market research to use your own assumptions as fact.
  Pendulum far left swing—very poor.

Scenario 2 – It is not sufficient to just ask friends and family when undertaking market research.
  Pendulum left swing—poor.

Scenario 3 – Market Research needs to contain extensive primary (field research) and secondary (desk research) to obtain the very best understanding of what your prospective customers want and need from your business.

Our artist has been face-to-face with a group of her prospective customers, interacted and engaged with them and has collected their feedback regarding their wants, needs, and demands in respect of her courses. By including appropriate start and finish times and networking coffee breaks in her offering, she has been successful in booking more courses.

Even better, she has spent time with two different groups (local college and U3A) of potential customers ensuring that she obtains the widest range of views to get consensus on her courses.

Pendulum far-right swing—Very Good

What would have made the market research excellent?

Our artist has received feedback from two of her initial target groups—Retired/Non-Work and Working/Evening Classes as members of these groups were attendees in her sample courses at the local College and the U3A.

However, there were no representatives of the school-aged target group she had considered, but many of the Working/Evening Classes attendees had children so she was able to get feedback from them. If she can get to engage with a group containing parents and children (perhaps booking a stall at a school fair) her market research swing would be far-right—excellent.

> **Bluebell Tip**
>
> Please be aware when proposing to work with children and vulnerable adults you will need a DBS check (Disclosure and Barring Service). For more information, please go to dbscheckonline.org.uk

However, Dianne had decided that having fully researched her first two target groups, and with the results giving her a great deal of confidence that she would be able to earn enough to meet her plans to work a three day week, that she would 'park' the school-aged target group to research further once she had started up her business.

So, once you have established what your target customers really want, and you have checked the strength of your market research 'swing' on our pendulum and it's far to the right, it's time to capture your notes and plans on our specially customised **Bluebell Market & Competitor Research worksheet** which you can download from the start of the chapter.

The one thing that market research cannot tell you is whether your prospective customers will actually buy your product or service.

You will only know that when they do, but you can be absolutely sure that the more thorough you have been in your market research and the better you have engaged with your potential customers, the greater the certainty that you will achieve your sales targets.

In our road map analogy, market research is similar to the research you undertake when you are choosing a destination to travel to. You need to find the very best match to ensure that when you reach the end of your journey you will be pleased with the place and the opportunities and benefits that are available to you.

This is exactly like finding a great match in your Customer Profile/Avatar groups when you find that they are the right people to appreciate your products or service and who want to do business with you.

Next, we will look at sales and customer service and how you can maximise your sales income…

CHAPTER 4

MARKETING—SALES & CUSTOMER SERVICE

Key Driver

> Documents to download for this chapter:
> Marketing—Sales and Customer Service Worksheet
> Bluebell Traditional Marketing Guide
> Events Calendar

Now you are clear who your customers are, it is time to consider how to promote your product or service to them. This is known as marketing.

Having spent time drawing up your target customer profiles, you will be able to consider the best way to contact these 'prospects'. This should reflect your market research findings and fulfil your prospective customers' needs. This is the foundation for the successful promotion and marketing of your product or service and it will ensure that you do not waste your marketing budget and valuable time.

One of the first things we would recommend that you do is to set up a website as your virtual shop window, even if you intend to have an actual shop. As we mentioned in Chapter 1, at the time of writing the Covid pandemic has taught us that it is good to have contingency options to continue your sales strategy whatever happens. In other years, the threat may be very different, but a business will always face challenges and it is good to be looking ahead for these and putting contingency plans in place to overcome them or, if that is not possible, to minimise the potential risk.

Selling from your website will be a very important part of your marketing strategy and your marketing message must be aimed at your identified target groups.

You can set up a website yourself. There are a number of providers for this, and most have guidance and tutorials to help you with the build. Alternatively, you can pay a website developer. We would recommend that you get a couple of quotes before making a decision.

For some entrepreneurs it is possible to start up a business without a website and save on costs. Social media channels such as Facebook (designed for friends and family) and Instagram (designed for lifestyle) etc., provide opportunities for service businesses, such as hair and beauty providers, to set up a business account and manage their customers online. They now also provide shop facilities.

Business professionals can use LinkedIn (business and employment oriented) to get their business up and running.

It is worth considering all possible options to get your message to your target audience.

For those with a website, the content will be critical as you develop and maintain it. Buyers will be searching for products and services, using various search engines (e.g., Google, Yahoo, Bing, etc.). Ideally, your website will need to show up in the top few search results. To achieve this, the content of your website needs to include keywords that potential customers might use to search the internet. These should be part of the organic content of your site, rather than just being placed at random, and they should link to your sales and service messages.

This is known as Search Engine Optimisation (SEO).

Understanding search engine optimisation and the digital world is a vast subject in its own right. We are, therefore, going to introduce you to a fabulous resource created by Google to develop your knowledge in this area. The vast majority of courses are free, and you can learn at your own pace.

Google Digital Garage

Google Digital Garage is a learning platform covering a range of digital marketing topics. It will enable you to choose the best social media platforms for your business and educate you on their use.

It also allows you to create your own individual learning plan on the platform and the tutorial style allows you to study in 'bitesize chunks'. Once you have created your website and social media platforms, you will need to carefully consider your marketing message:

Remember that your target audience is not everyone, it is the target groups that you have identified.

Your marketing proposition should be based on the following criteria:

- Advertise to the right customers using the right marketing channels, including a message which will appeal to them.
- Learn which kinds of media your target market customers will use so that you can contact them there.
- Create advertising which shows your potential customers how you can solve a problem they face, ease their lives, or save them time or money.

When promoting your product/service it is important to touch your potential customers' emotions and increase their desire for the product. A great tool to use to achieve this is called AIDA.

No, it's not an opera, it's a mnemonic! As we said previously, that's an aide-mémoire where the letters remind you of what is required. In this case:

A = Attention

The promotion, whether advert, flyer, Facebook post, blog, etc., should grab a buyer's attention. This may be via the colours used, an attention-grabbing picture, or words that 'hit home'.

I = Interest

Having grabbed attention, you now need to maintain the buyer's interest. This can be achieved by enticing words or maybe a discount offer or an introductory gift.

D = Desire

Now the buyer is interested, this is where their desire for the item can be ramped up by spelling out the benefits of owning the product.

A = Action

This is so important! Having attracted a customer with your promotion, you must guide them through to making a purchase. Your message must let your prospective customers know what to do next to get your product or service.

If your advert is online this can be achieved by having an online shop so that they can purchase straight away. Alternatively, provide an email address so that the buyer can order the item and leave their personal details so that you can complete the sale.

If the advert is on paper e.g., a leaflet, ensure that you include your email address and telephone number, web, and any social media addresses and, if appropriate, shop address and opening times.

You will see that we have advised under 'Desire' above that you should entice your prospective buyer by spelling out the <u>benefits</u> of buying your product or service. So how do you achieve this?

When engaging with your target audience, it is important to be clear about the difference between **the features** and **the benefits** when selling your product or service.

To illustrate—let us take sun cream as an example. The **features** of sun cream are the UV factor, the ingredients, if it is a spray or a cream, and whether it is waterproof. So, features are facts about your product or service, and they add credibility to your sales pitch.

However, the **benefits** of these features need to be shared with potential buyers as these explain how a product or service can improve their lives.

To easily differentiate between features and benefits, Just remember these three words:

"Which means that."

These three words are used to link up the features of your product or service to the benefits e.g.

> "You might be interested in this tablet as it contains factor X, **which means that** your headache will disappear within 5 minutes of taking it.

Let us imagine a sales discussion with a prospective customer, to illustrate the power of selling, using benefits as opposed to features:

> "You might be interested in this sun cream; it is a factor 30 and it is waterproof. You can buy it in a cream or a spray."

Or this one:

> "Here is our most popular sun cream. It is a factor 30 **which means that** you can stay in the sun for up to 2

hours before you need to top up. It is waterproof **so** it does not wash off if you have a swim and you can choose it in a spray or cream version, whichever you prefer. All the ingredients are hypoallergenic **which means that** If you have anyone in your family who has allergies, they will be safe using this cream.

You will see that selling the benefits of the product gives the customer much more information to make a positive buying decision.

To reiterate—the best way to sell the benefits is to use a phrase such as "which means that" or "so" to link the features to the benefits. This will increase a potential buyer's desire for your product.

As a small business owner, this is a very important aspect as you must concentrate on engaging with new customers, encouraging them to desire your product or service, and buy from you. Therefore, it is critical to understand your products, especially in a niche market, so that you can dominate them.

When you have your message clear in your mind, you will need to decide how best to promote your product or service. A mix of digital and traditional methods may be the appropriate route, but that is for your decide based on your research.

To help with the traditional marketing, we have provided a marketing pack for you to download from the link at the top of the page:

Bluebell Traditional Marketing Guide
Many new business owners fail to realise that a good service offering can massively improve sales. So, let's think about that for a minute. Why would that be?

Imagine that you are walking into a shop having seen a product in the window that you are interested in and would like to buy. The way that you are treated when you enter the establishment will make all the difference to whether you actually purchase the item or not, even though you feel the desire to take it home with you.

This would be the same if you see a product online that you really like, and then the process to buy it is long and complicated. The chances are that you will give up before you have managed to purchase the item.

What is going to differentiate your service?

- A smile when meeting a potential customer, either face to face or on the telephone (yes, it really does reflect in your voice!).
- A welcoming good morning/afternoon whether face to face or on the phone.
- Use of the customer's name (but not overuse!).
- Show interest in your customer. If you have to keep them waiting, apologise and keep them updated on how long you will be.
- Having good product knowledge and remembering to sell the benefits of your product or service.
- Deliver what you promise (best practice; make a note so you don't forget anything!).
- If you are corresponding online, keep your customer informed.
- Make sure that your online sales processes are welcoming and efficient.
- Thank your customer for their valued business.

In the event of a complaint or dissatisfied customer:

- Take your customer seriously.
- Say sorry.
- Get full details of the complaint.
- Agree timeframes for resolution.
- Aim to find a resolution that is acceptable to both parties.

> **Bluebell Tip**
>
> A customer who has made a complaint and had that complaint satisfactorily resolved will generally be extremely satisfied. They will remain as a customer, will be more likely to recommend the business to friends and family, and will repurchase from you.
>
> However, if the complaint remains unresolved, the former customer is likely to tell everyone who will listen how poor your company and products are.
>
> It is, therefore, worthwhile to spend time honing your customer service skills.
>
> Also, do not be afraid to say sorry. Many businesspeople will not say this to a customer thinking that it implies that they are at fault. A good way to say it is "I am very sorry to hear that you have a complaint. How may I aim to resolve it?"
>
> The customer will appreciate hearing the word sorry and you will know exactly what they hope for in terms of a resolution.

Please do not underestimate how important your service offering is when dealing with your customers!

Now that we have looked at several sales and service tactics, it is time to download our Bluebell Business Marketing—Sales and service Worksheet from the link at the start of the chapter and decide exactly how you intend to create sales and service excellence in your new business.

Ensure that you include an events calendar within your plan to take advantage of any key events e.g., shows, and key dates including Valentines, Easter, Diwali, Christmas, and any other occasions appropriate to your business.

Remember that your plan should be simple, focused, and effective. What you are aiming to do is:

Attract new customers.
Up-sell to increase sales revenue. Think McDonalds, "Would you like fries with that?" Can we make it into a meal?

Get customers to repurchase from you.
Keep your valued customers for life.
Make your customers fans so they recommend you to friends and family.

> ### Bluebell Tip
>
> It is many times harder to find new customers than to retain your existing customers so please ensure that you have a great process in place to achieve this.

How successful is your marketing activity?

Whilst you are writing your Marketing—Sales and Service plan, there is another area that you will need to consider. To protect any marketing budget that you put in place and to ensure that you get a good return on your marketing investment, you must keep a close eye on your marketing activity and tactics to see how successful they are proving to be. This is known as (**return on investment or ROI**). To do this you will need to keep a note of all your marketing costs and all income earned via each sales tactic or activity. You will quickly see which tactics are creating sales and those that are not as successful. It is important that you review tactics regularly. We would recommend every one to two months depending on the level of marketing activity that you are undertaking. If you find that tactics are not working for you, you can then rethink and end the activity early, or revise and devise a more successful tactic. This way you will not be wasting time or money.

> ### Bluebell Tip
>
> To ensure a robust review, you may wish to use codes. For example, you have items for sale online and you intend to attract customers with an introductory discount. Ask buyers to enter the code you have chosen for that sales tactic e.g. DO3 (discount online 3) to trigger the discount. This will mean that they are happy to do that and it helps you to see which tactic or offer is most attractive at that time.
>
> It is also helpful, whenever possible, to get feedback from buyers to understand where they have heard about your business. This information is very valuable for future marketing campaigns!
>
> If your business has a seasonal element, you will also need to take this into account during your reviews and it will be beneficial to consider how you will best deal with seasonal peaks and dips in sales.
>
> You will learn about the improvement circle process in Chapter 8, which will help with all of your reviews.

We would recommend Google Analytics as an excellent free analysis tool to use alongside your ROI reviews. It is a web analysis tool that will give you lots of information about traffic to your website. Users can track website activity such as how long visitors have stayed on your site, what pages they have looked at, along with information on the source of the traffic.

You will first need to have a Google account and then go to Google Analytics.

Google Analytics

Press the sign-up button at the top right of the home page and provide the basic information required for the website you want to monitor. You will receive a tracking code to paste onto your pages, so Google knows when your site is visited. In a few hours, you will be able to see data about your site.

Google provides a Help Centre so you will get all the information you require once you start using the tool. It is really helpful in understanding if your marketing is successful in driving customers to your website.

In this chapter, we have signposted you to Google Digital Garage for digital marketing ideas and tactics and have provided our Bluebell traditional marketing sheet too. This is so as not to swamp you with too much detail and allow you to create your own customised plan.

This is an important chapter, and if you use the tried and tested tools we have included to help your sales and service dialogue come alive, we expect you to do very well!

Having now thought about your brand, your customer avatars, and your sales and service tactics, we will now have a closer look at you as the business owner…

CHAPTER 5

PERSONAL CHARACTER & SKILLS ANALYSIS (SWOC)—ANALYSING YOUR PERSONAL SKILLS AND ABILITIES

ABILITIES

Key Driver

> **Bluebell Documents to download for this Chapter:**
> **Personal Character & Skills Analysis (SWOC) and Action Plan**
> **Personal Character & Skills Analysis (SWOC) Example**

We have included these worksheets in your business plan pack, but what are they? Well, they are documents that allow you to assess your own **strengths** and any **weaknesses** in respect of running your proposed business. They allow you to consider what skills you have, which will be of benefit to your business, or find any areas where your skills are not strong, or potentially missing altogether. They also allow you to list any available **opportunities** you can take advantage of and any personal **concerns** you may have about your enterprise.

Going through these worksheets will really help you to fully consider your motives for starting up your business and answer some key questions regarding your personal preparation. <u>The outcome will be clarity for you via an action plan so that you can address any shortfalls and maintain and amplify your strengths.</u>

How do you start?

Download the <u>Bluebell Personal Character and Skills Analysis (SWOC) and Example</u> from the links at the beginning of the chapter.

We discussed this concept in Chapter 1, and now is the time to look at it in more detail. Let's consider the questions we posed in the 'Brand You' Chapter listed again below:

- Why do you want to go into business? E.g., New beginning, improved lifestyle.
- What experience (if any) do you have to support a new business?
- What skills can you bring to the business which will make the journey easier?
- What skills do you need to learn? E.g., Organisational skills both personal and business (as the two are inextricably linked).
- Are your finances strong to get you through the first few months or perhaps you have had money problems in the past and your financial track record isn't the best?
- How much money do you need to earn from the business to cover your personal living expenses?

- Do you have confidence that you have got 'what it takes' or do you have low self-esteem or a lack of self-belief?

It is now time for you to fill in the Personal Character and Skills Analysis (SWOC) form putting your answers and thoughts about the above questions under the appropriate heading for you, depending on whether it is a strength, weakness, opportunity, or concern. If you have any other matter personal to you, which has not been mentioned, please add it to your SWOC.

In addition, to help you to think more widely, we have included an EXAMPLE personal SWOC for you to download. It shows how a mechanic proposing a new mobile mechanic business completed his. It aims to give you some areas to consider, but please note that this exercise is personal to you, so it will only add value to your business plan if you are honest in your answers.

We are looking for KEY areas on this form so would expect you to have a maximum of 3 points in each quadrant. These will be the areas that you will need to work on first.

The aim is to produce an action plan for you to work on during the first 12 months of your business.

Here is an extract of the Example SWOC:

Bluebell Business — Enabling Business Growth
EXAMPLE
Personal Character SWOC ANALYSIS

My Personal Strengths	My Personal Weaknesses
• I have worked as a mechanic for 20 years and have just been made redundant. I am ready to set up my own mobile mechanic business, so I feel confident that I will do well. • My time keeping is excellent, as is my sickness record. • I enjoy dealing with customers.	• I have never run a business before. How do I ensure that I can meet all legal requirements? I have no knowledge of this. • I can lack confidence in certain situations. I tend to back away from conflict. • I am not very organised
My Personal Opportunities	**My Personal Concerns**

> ### Bluebell Tip
>
> This form will allow you to look closely at yourself, what you have to offer your business, and where you might have character or skill gaps.
>
> It is a snapshot of you at a particular moment in time. You can re-do this exercise whenever you wish, to reassess your progress, and if your action plan has been successful, you will find that you have different areas to work on each time. It ensures that you are applying continuous improvement principles to you, the brand leader.

> Let's summarise:
>
> 1. Download Personal Character and Skills Analysis (SWOC)
> 2. Answer the bullet point questions and add any other information which you consider relevant to your SWOC. Place each answer in the appropriate quadrant depending on whether it is a strength, weakness, opportunity, or concern for you.
> 3. Read Example SWOC and jot down any thoughts that arise for your personal SWOC.
> 4. You should have no more than 3 key areas that you wish to consider/address under each subject heading.
> 5. You will then need to review your completed SWOC and consider which items are development/improvement areas for you, and which you will need to tackle first. You have to prioritise as you will only be able to work on a couple of these development needs at the same time as setting up your business, so choose ones that will have the greatest impact!
> 6. Add these subjects to your action plan which is on page 2 of your SWOC.
> 7. We have included action plan ideas and best practices below to assist you.

So as summarised above, once you have finished, it is then time to consider what your SWOC is telling you. **Please listen to it!**

Some generic thoughts:

> **Strengths** – Be proud of these. You should plan to embrace and strengthen them.

How will you maintain them?

Weaknesses – We all have personal skills or character areas that are not as strong. Aim to identify yours and decide what steps you can take to improve them or minimise their effect. Do you have the key skills you will need? If not, make a note of them on your SWOC.

Opportunities – These are beneficial for you. How will you make the most of them and use them to your advantage?

Concerns – These will no doubt be at the forefront of your mind. How can you overcome them and put your mind at rest?

Let's now look more closely at some of the subjects that may have featured on your SWOC. We cannot cover every eventuality here, so we have chosen to cover subjects that new entrepreneurs regularly mention.

As we said, the aim is for you to now develop a SWOC action plan which will form a critical part of your business planning documents. Our personal SWOC worksheet has an action plan on page 2 for you to complete once you have decided what action you need to take.

Strengths

- **Years of experience in a subject relevant to your business**

Maintain this strength via continuous professional development.

Add appropriate training/self-learning to your action plan.

This is particularly important if you have a qualification to maintain.

- **A good sickness/attendance record**

This is great for your new business as unless you are employing staff your customers will be dependent on you.

You may wish to consider getting accident and sickness insurance to provide you with an income in case you are ill.

<u>Please always get advice on an appropriate product from an insurance broker or your bank.</u>

- **You enjoy dealing with customers.**

This is a great strength to have, and once you have your own business, you will need to develop processes for each customer interaction to maximise your customers' experience and gain customer engagement.

Weaknesses

- **Lack of knowledge of start-up formalities**

There is a great deal of support for start-up businesspeople today and many organisations which have been specially set up to support them. Searching start-up business support and including your local area in the search will bring up helpful results.

In the UK, The British Chambers of Commerce are a network of local chambers that support all businesses, large and small, and provide a wide range of help and advice for start-ups. They are a 'catch all' in terms of professional advice tailored to your business to ensure that you have all legal obligations in place, and nothing is missed.

They provide face to face support through business adviser meetings, mentor engagement, training courses, workshops, help with finding grant funding and can signpost you to other relevant agencies, where appropriate.

The support of your local chamber will help you to create a solid foundation for your business.

We highly recommend that you book a face to face appointment with your local chamber, and we have added a section in our business plan documents so that you will not forget this important step.

We are proud to have worked with our local Chambers of Commerce in Staffordshire and we are members.

Please browse their website in the link below, to get an understanding of what most local chambers offer:
https://staffordshirechambers.co.uk/

Find your local chamber here:
https://britishchambers.org.uk

Other agencies:
Business Innovation Centres

These are centres where you can get specialist help and support with innovative products and services and some of the centres have 'easy let' office and workshop accommodation. You will need to search Business Innovation Centres on the Internet and look for one near to you as there isn't an overall link.

Our local Business Innovation Centre is:
Staffordshire Business Innovation Centre

The Princes Trust
https://princes-trust.org.uk
Local university business schools.

You can see then that this weakness can be easily overcome with the correct specialist advice and guidance, as it is merely a lack of knowledge that can soon be rectified.

- **Poor organisational skills**

This is a critical area for an entrepreneur, both personally and in respect of your business (as you will have to manage both). Luckily, these are skills that can be readily learned and will soon become a strength.

The key skills to learn to become organised and productive are diary and to-do list management. Many of the best practice ideas we shared with you in Chapter 2—Business Planning will help you to achieve this.

We recommend that you get an A4 Notebook and an A4 Diary (readily obtainable for a few pounds) or you may prefer to use one of the many specially designed organiser planners or phone apps which are available. Whichever you chose, it is the way you use them which will help to make you organised.

Get into the habit of keeping notes of business meetings and compiling to-do lists of actions that you need to undertake. If you write everything down and review outstanding items regularly, you will soon become organised. Begin using your diary to manage your appointments. Block out time slots to prepare for meetings and aim to get to appointments ahead of the arranged time. This is not only courteous, but it makes a good impression on those you are meeting, you will appear very organised, and your customer service skills will be enhanced.

- **Lack of confidence**

This can be a challenge for new entrepreneurs. There are many excellent books on this subject that would help but we have found that a good way to overcome fears is role-playing. Ask someone that you trust to help you prepare for your new business owner role. First, make a list of the situations which you would be nervous about facing e.g., a customer complaint. Start by playing the customer's role and let your helper play the business owner then switch. Repeat as often as necessary. As you go through this process you will start to understand how to deal with the customer and how to achieve the best outcome. Please don't let the first time you deal with this situation be with a real customer!

> ### Bluebell Tip
>
> As we said in the last chapter, in this situation do not be afraid to say sorry. Many businesspeople will not say this to a customer thinking that it implies that they are at fault. A good way to say it is: "I am very sorry to hear that you have a complaint. How may I aim to resolve it?"
>
> The customer will appreciate hearing the word sorry and you will know exactly what they hope for in terms of a resolution.

Opportunities

- **Flexible hours and holidays**

A real opportunity here! Many new business owners are looking at flexible hours as a reason for becoming self-employed. This can be achieved as a business owner has more authority over when he/she starts and finishes work and can take more leave than people in employment do. However, it is worth mentioning that for sole traders who have no staff, it is important to choose holiday dates early in the year and mark them clearly in your work diary. This will ensure that appointments are not made by mistake in a holiday week causing customer upset when the appointment must be cancelled. Again, flexible hours must be clearly marked. Diary management is both an organisational skill and a customer service skill and will also be a major benefit for your business if you get it right.

- **Training**

Again, the business support agencies can provide a lot of help and support here. There are a range of free and low-cost courses available for start-up business owners. A word of warning though, **there is a balance to maintain between building your knowledge and building your business, especially in the first year.** Whilst you are training, you will not be available to see customers, and this will affect your income earning potential. This coupled with the potential cost of the courses will have an impact on your cash flow.

Please then consider your personal training requirements carefully, prioritising continuing professional development (if appropriate) to maintain qualifications and then consider your skill gaps and business training requirements. Please schedule these very carefully into your action plan whilst keeping an eye on your costs.

A reminder of the link for online marketing training which you may wish to add to your action plan:

Google Digital Garage

Google Digital Garage caters for an individual's personal development in addition to other skills-based training e.g., How to increase productivity at work (become better at managing your time and learn how delegation and prioritisation can help you work more efficiently), and effective networking (learn how networking can help you grow your business).

Concerns

- **Keeping your books and other records.**

This is a worry for many new business owners, but help is available.

There is a requirement to keep records of your income and expenditure as a self-employed person as you have to submit an annual tax return so that you can pay any tax and national insurance that is due.

GOV.UK set out rules relating to business records, and you can do no better than to follow the instructions on their website. Here is the link:

https://www.gov.uk/self-employed-records

They also offer guidance on how long you must keep your records on the same link.

It is very important to be disciplined when keeping a record of your business income and expenses. In previous years, you may have decided to use a cash book or a simple spreadsheet. However, HM Revenue and Customs have now introduced a change to the tax system, known as Making Tax Digital. The aim is to make tax administration more effective, more efficient, and simpler for taxpayers. When Making Tax Digital is fully rolled out, computer software must be used to complete your accounts.

You may be entitled to free accounts software from your bank when you open a business account. **We like Free Agent, which is an excellent bookkeeping app, currently available free from NatWest to business customers, and linked to your business bank account.** For non-customers, there is a charge.

Have a look at this video to see Free Agent in action with a NatWest new business customer:

<u>NatWest business customer using Free Agent</u>

Here is the link if you decide to sign up:

<u>Free Agent via NatWest</u>

<u>Other banks have offerings e.g., Barclays have an app with an invoicing facility and others including HSBC will allow you to sync your bank entries direct to your software, including the software packages mentioned below.</u>

There are paid software packages available on the market too, such as QuickBooks, Xero, Sage, amongst others. It is important to choose whichever one feels right for you as this will ensure that you will keep your books up to date. All have tutorials and help facilities to get you started.

If you update your accounts each week, you will be able to track your profits/losses. You can keep on top of things and react quickly when necessary. It is also much easier to remember items when you have only just dealt with them rather than trying to remember them after a few months.

Will I earn enough to support my family?

This is a real concern for many new entrepreneurs. The first step in this process is to clearly understand exactly how much you need to keep your family for a minimum of 12 months. We are pleased to advise that we have an excellent Business Planning tool to introduce to you which will give you the answer! Our version is called <u>Bluebell Personal Survival Budget</u> and we will be introducing it to you in the next chapter. Meanwhile, just be assured that we can assist in putting put your mind at rest on this subject.

- **How much income will my business need to generate to cover all of its financial commitments?**

This is a critical question and again we have a Business Planning tool that will provide you with an excellent steer on the income that you need to generate in the first 12 months. Our version is called <u>Bluebell Business 'First Time' Cashflow Forecast.</u> We will assist you in completing the form and working out your business finance requirements in Chapter 7. Again, peace of mind!

- **How can I gain enough customers to make my business a success?**

This is a great question and one that any start-up business owner will want to be reassured about.

The answer is that this is largely down to the business itself, the products or services on offer, and the extent to which the business owner has researched their marketplace and competitors. In addition, the business brand itself is a key element together with the standard of customer service interactions.

We have aimed to design this book to fully answer this question and then it is over to you to achieve the results that you are planning for. The stronger the research and thought that you have put into your business plan, the more likely your business will be successful.

We have now looked in detail at the Bluebell Business Character and Skills Analysis (SWOC) and given you information regarding the key aspects that most new business owners need help with when starting up their business. You will find much more detail throughout the book to build upon what you have learned here.

Let's now think about our road map analogy. The Personal Character and Skills Analysis (SWOC) relates to the skills and abilities of the businessowner, the person 'at the wheel' of the business—the driver. Does the business owner have the necessary skills and drive they need to get the business up and running and get to their destination, or will they need someone else 'on board' to help with the journey?

This is where you can consider if you need to get, or if necessary, buy in help if you don't currently have the skills you need. That may be a bookkeeper or a social media expert, or someone else with appropriate skills to assist with tasks whilst you get on with the 'driving'. The SWOC action plan will help you to confirm if you can drive alone or if you need help on the way.

Once you have completed your <u>Personal Character & Skills Analysis (SWOC) and Action Plan</u> please put it with your business planning paperwork. However, you may want to wait to complete your action plan until you have finished reading through the book, as we have lots more helpful information to come!

Our next step is to look at the <u>Bluebell Personal Survival Budget</u> planning document in Chapter 6.

This is the first of our financial documents.

CHAPTER 6

FINANCIALS - PERSONAL SURVIVAL BUDGET—HOW MUCH WILL YOU NEED TO DRAW FROM YOUR BUSINESS?

> **Bluebell Document to Download for this Chapter.**
> **Personal Survival Budget (PSB)**

Now that we have looked at the non-financial areas of the business plan, it is time to turn to money matters, both personal and business-related.

In this chapter, we cover one of the core elements of your business plan—the Bluebell Business Personal Survival Budget (PSB)

So, what is it?

It allows you to calculate how much you spend monthly and annually on your personal/ household day to day living expenses.

We are always surprised how little attention the personal survival budget gets by so many starting up in business, but this document is vital to business success.

Why is it so important?

There is an inseparable link between your business expenditure and your personal expenditure. The reason is very simple; your business has to generate enough profit to allow you to draw funds to cover your personal expenditure, in addition to all your business expenses. In many cases, it can be your business's largest expense.

Completing this document fully, covering everything that you need to spend personally in a 12-month period, is so important. Nothing must be missed out! Expenditure that comes annually, for example, Christmas, Easter, and birthday costs must be included, and the total divided by 12 to calculate how much you will need to pay yourself each month to cover your survival budget requirements. We will explain this in more detail in Chapter 7 when we look at the Bluebell Business 'First Time' Cashflow forecast.

We must stress again that everything you spend personally must be accounted for in this document. If the personal survival budget isn't completed in this way, when it comes to setting your pricing (again see chapter 7), it will be wrong and it is very difficult to increase prices once they have been set.

Having emphasised the importance of this document, we must say that some people find it quite challenging to complete and are often shocked and occasionally concerned when they see the results. This is because most of us have little idea how much we spend annually on living expenses, eating out, and other household costs. The shock can be greater for those who may be struggling from a financial perspective.

You will see then, the benefit of spending time working through this form, to ensure that you are fully aware of how much you will need to draw from your new business to keep your household going. This will ensure that your pricing is accurate and not understated.

> **Bluebell Tip**
> If you would appreciate help with your personal finances, you can contact a free, impartial organisation that specialises in financial guidance such as the Money Advice Service. Please see the link below:
>
> Money Advice Service - Citizensadvice.org.uk
>
> Most banks will give help and guidance to their personal customers regarding money matters. This may be advice via their mobile phone apps or face to face.

Please now have a look at the document itself by downloading it from the link at the beginning of the chapter. Here is an extract:

Personal Survival Budget

Key:
- Cells auto-calculate
- Enter your own values

Household expenses	Notes	Monthly expenses (£)	Yearly expenses (£)
Mortgage or rent		£0.00	£0.00
Council Tax		£0.00	£0.00
Water bill		£0.00	£0.00
Gas and Electricity		£0.00	£0.00
House property and contents insurances		£0.00	£0.00
Personal Insurances (Life, Health, Dentist etc)		£0.00	£0.00
Food and general household supplies		£0.00	£0.00
Prescriptions & medication		£0.00	£0.00
House maintenance and repairs		£0.00	£0.00
Clothing		£0.00	£0.00
Landline Telephone, Broadband etc		£0.00	£0.00
Mobile (s)		£0.00	£0.00
Sky, BT, Virgin, Netflix etc		£0.00	£0.00
TV licence		£0.00	£0.00

You will see that the personal survival budget document caters for most of the common expenses people incur, but we would encourage you to personalise it and make it bespoke for you. Please do not guess figures unless you really have to. The information will be so much more robust if you look at bank statements and other financial records to get the information as accurate as possible.

You will see that there is a section at the bottom of the personal survival budget which relates to household income. So, what's that? Well, you will need to account for any other income which may come into your household. This may already be in place or may commence once you start your new business. For example, it may be that you will stay on in your current job for a few hours a week whilst your business gets up and running. You may take on a part-time job (often called a side hustle) to help your finances in the first year of starting up your business. It may be that your spouse or partner is employed and contributing to your household expenses. Whatever personal income stream (outside of your business) that will continue once you have started up your business, add it to this form in the household income section.

(A word of warning for those of you who intend to take on part time work in year one of your business as a buffer, or if you are continuing to work in your current job as you get your business started; If these additional income streams are only to be short term, **please do not include them in your PSB** as this has implications for your pricing as you will see below and in Chapter 7.)

Having calculated your personal annual living expenses, and any potential additional income which you will have available, you will understand exactly how much reliance there will be on your business once you start to trade.

Note that this is an important part of the pricing process!

As we mentioned earlier, new entrepreneurs often omit this stage in the business planning process. Please do not go down that route unless you have a really accurate idea of your monthly household spend.

Remember that this is one of the core elements to make your business a success and is a great exercise for anyone to undertake to get a better understanding of their household outgoings.

> ## Bluebell Tip
>
> ### Here is an interesting thought!
>
> Now that we have covered the basic personal survival budget, we have a suggestion. In your first year of business, you will be planning to cover your living expenses and get your business up and running—effectively covering the basics. However, it is good to also start to think about your own well-being going forward.
>
> Whilst we are at the planning stage, why not undertake an aspirational personal survival budget, adding in the cost of an additional holiday, a gym membership, or a creative course, for example. Whatever takes your fancy.
>
> So, what is an aspirational personal survival budget? Well, it is the same as the basic exercise that we have just described, except that you are going to add in personal expenditure that will add to your happiness and well-being. We call this the 'feel good' factor. For example, if you want two holidays a year, add them in. This is the section where you ask yourself what will make you happy in life and cater for it.
>
> This may not be possible in year one, but if you have developed an aspirational survival budget, you will have a clear idea of what you need to achieve—maybe in year two? It is a great opportunity to carefully consider whilst you are in the planning stage. You can then aim to manage your business to create the additional income required to achieve this.
>
> Note: If you do decide to take an additional holiday, you will need to take into account the cost of your absence from the business (e.g., reduced sales) in addition to the cost of the holiday.

Now that you know how much you need to earn as a minimum to cover your personal living expenses, we will look at your proposed business's finance requirements.

CHAPTER 7

CASH FLOW FORECASTING— HOW MUCH MONEY WILL FLOW THROUGH YOUR BUSINESS?

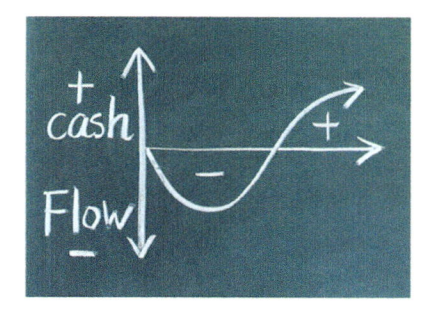

Key Driver

> **Bluebell documents available to download for this Chapter:**
> **Basic Cashflow Forecast**
> **Dianne's 'First Time' Cashflow Forecasts**
> **Budget v Actual Cashflow Forecast**

When we decided to write this book, we expressed in our mission statement that we would make it simple, focused, and effective. This was to enable our readers to understand the key components of a start-up business and show them how all the planning elements fit together to give their business every chance of success.

We acknowledge that dealing with business finance for the first time can be complex and is certainly bespoke, as everyone's circumstances are different and require individual consideration.

It is for this reason we recommend that you, as a startup business owner, seek advice from a qualified accountant so you can discuss your business finances in conjunction with your individual circumstances. This is essential as there isn't one model that fits all.

Many accountants will provide an initial consultation free of charge, and this will ensure that all financial aspects, both business and personal, will be considered ahead of the business start-up.

So, to keep this chapter as simple, focused, and effective as we can, we are going to take you through it via a sole trader who has income from her business only, who aligns her trading year with the tax year i.e., accounts prepared to 5th April annually, and is not VAT registered (learn more about VAT in Chapter 8). So many new businesses start in this way, and we feel using this model will help provide clarity for you.

In this chapter, we have three key financial documents to present to you, together with important information relating to each of these documents.

Before we start, we want to make you aware that many new entrepreneurs feel really challenged when they are first presented with a cash flow forecast. It may be because of the financial implications, the strings of numbers, or just the unknown.

We aim to help you understand the importance of these documents within your business and to familiarise you with their use, so that they become friends and allies along your business journey.

The three documents are very similar but are used in different ways. **As a result, this chapter will look different from the rest of the book as we have put the information into individual sections to keep the message as clear as possible.**

Our recommendations for this chapter:

- Download the following four documents from the links at the top of the page

    Basic cash flow forecast
    Dianne's "First time" cash flow forecasts
    Budget versus actual cash flow forecast

- Sign up for a software accounting package compatible with making tax digital
- Open a business bank account and a business savings account

Understanding Tax, National Insurance & Net Profit

Before we embark on the cash flow elements of this module, it is important that you fully understand what net profit is, as it will be an integral part of your cash flow forecasting in terms of making provision for tax and national insurance and your business financial reports.

Self-employed business owners currently pay **income tax** and **two types of national insurance** to HM Revenue and Customs (HMRC) based on **net profit** made by the business in each individual tax year. **You will report these figures to HM Revenue and Customs via an annual Self-Assessment return.** Here are Government links so that you can see the current rates:

self-employed-national-insurance-rates – GOV.UK
Income Tax rates and Personal Allowances – GOV.UK

For you to make monthly provision for income tax and national insurance in your cash flow forecast, you will need to calculate the net profit your business will make every month.

This will then allow you to use HMRC's tax calculator to work out how much tax and national insurance you will expect to pay so you can then make provision to put money aside every month to pay HMRC when these payments become due.

We will start the explanation of net profit with the illustration below:

Business income in the tax year	£25000
Minus the **allowable** business expenses in the tax year	£10000
Net profit for the tax year (which is taxable)	£15000

The way to work out net profit is very easy as per the example above. The allowable business expenses in the tax year are subtracted from the business income for the tax year and this gives you the net profit for the tax year.

Again, referring to the example above, it is clear that the higher the allowable business expenses figure is the lower the net profit will be and because the amount of tax and national insurance paid is based on the net profit, the business will pay less tax and national insurance. This is effective tax planning. It is, therefore, important to ensure that you record all of your allowable business expenses.

But what are allowable business expenses?

There are two types of business expenses:

1. **Allowable** business expenses
2. **Non-allowable** business expenses

The first thing to say here is that the vast majority of your business expenses will be allowable business expenses.

Allowable business expenses are those expenses **you are allowed to use in the calculation of the net profit for tax purposes.**

Non-allowable business expenses **are not allowed to be used when calculating the net profit.**

Please see the government links below which explain and specify allowable and non-allowable expenses.

Expenses if you are self-employed - GOV.UK
What expenses can I claim in my self-assessment tax return? GOV.UK

You will see from the government links above **that money taken from your business to pay for private purchases is non-allowable**.

This means that the **business owners wage (known as drawings and calculated from the personal survival budget) is a non-allowable business expense. It is really important to remember this.**

Contact the Self-Assessment General Enquiries at HMRC if you're not sure whether a business cost is an allowable expense

Now that we are clear about NET PROFIT and why it is important in building cash flow forecasts, let's look at cash flow itself and start to understand what it means.

Understanding Cash flow

Cash flow is the flow of cash into and out of your business to keep your business operating.

A positive cash flow (i.e., more money going into the business than goes out of the business) is vital for business success. This is known as liquidity.

By contrast, a negative cash flow (i.e., more money going out of the business than goes into the business) means the business will not survive as the business will be insolvent (unable to pay debts owed).

It, therefore, goes without saying that a positive cash flow is vital and enables the business to meet all its financial commitments and develop and grow.

A cashflow forecast document in its most simple and basic form is a spreadsheet. This document is used to **forecast** the flow of money in and out of a business each month, over a specific period, usually 12 months. For the forecast to be produced, the business owner is required to predict the business income to be received by the business, each month. Then to calculate what business expenditure will be necessary over the same period.

To achieve this, the business owner must carefully consider any business seasonality which could affect sales income e.g., in a gardening business, where summer income may be very different to winter income. Also, to take account of any credit terms offered to customers e.g., payment 10 days after invoice, or by suppliers e.g., payment 30 days from delivery, as these options would defer the due payment dates of incoming and outgoing payments. Having completed this exercise, **the business owner can clearly see if there will be specific times across the year where there will be 'pinch points' where expenditure is greater than income.** Knowing when this might happen in your business and being able to think of prior solutions ahead of those times, makes the cash flow forecast a key management tool and invaluable for a business owner.

Why does a business need a cash flow forecast?

The whole point of completing a cash flow forecast is that you can see into the future of your business (for the period forecast) and understand, from your best predictions, exactly how the cash will flow, to keep your business alive. You will recall that we advised that a business plan is like a road map for a journey, and the cash flow is the document that gives you a 'heads up' that you might run out of 'fuel' (i.e., cash) on the way. Knowing this in advance allows you to find solutions e.g., to improve sales from the figures predicted, agree credit terms with a supplier to defer due payment dates, approach your bank for support, amongst others. If you hadn't completed your cash flow forecast, the first indication of a problem might be your bank declining a payment to a supplier! As it is, you will be made aware of those 'pinch points' as soon as you see minus figures in your net cash flow.

It is also worth knowing that a cash flow forecast can be a useful predictive tool to test various scenarios for your business e.g., introducing a new product line.

Introducing our Bluebell basic cash flow document

Please refer to the downloaded Bluebell basic cash flow
The layout of a cash flow forecast

A cash flow forecast has three main sections:

Cash In – Cash flowing into the business each month.
Cash Out – Payments flowing out of the business each month.
Net cash flow – The cash flowing into the business each month minus the business expenditure each month.

Let's now have a look at the document itself!
We are now going to break the cash flow document down into three sections for ease of explanation. We are showing three months only.

Part 1
Cash in – Business income:

Income	Pre-start Up	MONTH 1	MONTH 2	MONTH 3
Business Income				
Loans				
Grants				
Capital Introduced				
(A) Total Income	£0.00	£0.00	£0.00	£0.00

This section shows the business income projected to be received into the business. Business income is always recorded in the month the business **expects** to receive the money.

There are occasions when the business may receive other income from non-trading sources; for example, grants, bank loans or personal funds that the business owner is introducing into the business to get the ball rolling. These funds are recorded on separate lines to the business income and again are recorded in the month when the funds are **expected** into the business.

Part 2
Cash out – Business expenditure:

This section has a list of several types of payments likely to be made by a business. Projected business outgoings should be shown against the appropriate payment type. The cash flow forecast should reflect the month that the business **expects** to make payments out of its bank account.

Business Expenditure	Pre-start Up	MONTH 1	MONTH 2	MONTH 3
Stock Purchases				
Business Insurance				
Business Mileage				
Stationery & Postage				
Marketing				
Business Mobile				
Accountancy Fees				
Bank Charges				
Provision for Tax & NI				
Owners Wages (Drawings)				
Loan Repayments				
Loan Interest				
(B) Total Expenditure	£0.00	£0.00	£0.00	£0.00
A - B		£0.00	£0.00	£0.00	£0.00
Balance B/Forward		£0.00	£0.00	£0.00	£0.00

Once you have entered these figures into the cash flow spreadsheet it will auto calculate the totals for you.

Part 3
Cash in the Business - Net cash flow

A - B	£0.00	£0.00	£0.00	£0.00
Balance B/Forward	£0.00	£0.00	£0.00	£0.00
Cash in the Business	£0.00	£0.00	£0.00	£0.00

(A – B): Net cash flow
The net cash flow is the income received for the month minus the business expenditure paid out for the month.

Balance B/Forward
This is the amount of cash left in the business at the end of the previous month which is brought forward to the beginning of the following month.

Cash in the business:
This is the amount of cash remaining in the business at the end of each month and is a key figure for any business owner to observe, especially if any of the monthly figures in the period predicted are negative, i.e., more money has gone out of the business than was available!

Bluebell 'first-time' cash flow document

To be clear, the first time cash flow forecast document is the basic cash flow document, but the income line is renamed as income target in the 'first time' cash flow forecast. It is the method used to complete the forms which differentiate them.

As we explained in Section 2, preparing a basic cash flow document for a start-up business entrepreneur can be a bit overwhelming, as it requires that several assumptions need to be made as to how the business will progress, income-wise, in its first year of trade.

For this reason, we have developed our 'first-time' cash flow forecast.

We would expect you to use the 'first time' cash flow document in the planning stage of the business.

The first time cash flow forecast will give you, as the business owner, a steer on:

1. Providing an income target to ensure that all monthly business expenses are met (coloured yellow).
2. Allowing you, as the business owner, to take the 'wage' you require (known as drawings for sole traders) as calculated in Chapter 6 – Personal Survival Budget (coloured pink).
3. Ensuring that you save so that you can pay your income tax and national insurance when it is due (coloured turquoise).
4. A pricing strategy guide (coloured purple).
5. The hours you will need to work if you are a service provider or wish to work part-time (coloured purple).

So, how do we produce this 'first-time' cash flow forecast?
To start the ball rolling, here are two positioning statements:

- "It is challenging to predict the business **income** for year one."
- "It is possible to predict and be quite accurate about the business **expenses** for year one."

Therefore, the rationale behind our first-time cash flow forecast is to allow you to create a monthly **income target** for your new business by adding together all of your monthly business expenses.

So why would you want to do this?

Well, if you can be clear about what expenses your business will have to cover throughout its first year, you will have a monthly income target to aim for. This covers:

1. Your own wage, as the business owner, known as drawings (and outlined in your personal survival budget).
2. Your tax and national insurance commitments, as the business owner, which will become due to HM Revenue and Customs.
3. All your other business expenses.

Knowing this figure will be extremely comforting for you as the business owner. It will be an essential piece of information to help guide you in the early months of your business.

To illustrate how to complete a "first-time" cash flow forecast we are going to refer back to Chapter 3 – Market Research and show you how our artist Dianne went about completing hers.

For ease of illustration, we are only using three months of the full twelve months cash flow forecast. The monthly figures will, of course, be the same for the remaining nine months.

You will see that there are three cash flow forecast extracts—the reason for this is to clearly illustrate the method of completion of Dianne's 'first-time' cash flow forecast.

You will see that Dianne has itemised her expected business expenses for the year and spread them evenly over the 12 months. An expense that is due to be paid by the business annually i.e., only once in the year **(on this 'first-time cash flow only)** is divided by 12 so that a monthly figure can be inserted. She also included her monthly wage (drawings required to cover her personal survival budget).

Income	Pre-start Up	MONTH 1	MONTH 2	MONTH 3
Income target		1877	1877	1877
	£0.00			
(A) Total Income	£0.00	£1,877.00	£1,877.00	£1,877.00

Expenditure	Pre-start Up	MONTH 1	MONTH 2	MONTH 3
Art materials		120	120	120
Business insurance		16	16	16
web hosting		11	11	11
Business mobile		30	30	30
Marketing		100	100	100
Diannes wage		1600	1600	1600
Provision for Tax & NI				
(B) Total costs	£0.00	£1,877.00	£1,877.00	£1,877.00

You will see that by doing this, Dianne has total monthly business expenses of £1877 and a minimum income target of £1877 (line B total costs) but she still needs to make monthly provisions for the tax and national insurance she will have to pay.

Dianne now reflected back to her market research to consider whether her income target was achievable.

Having reflected on her market research, Dianne felt able to increase her monthly income target to £2300, feeling confident that this was achievable.

She now added this figure to her first-time cash flow forecast to reflect this new income target, but she still needed to make provision for tax and national insurance.

First of all, Dianne needs to work out her monthly net profit as shown below: The calculation for Dianne's monthly net profit is:

Business Income	£2300
Minus the allowable business expenses	£277
Monthly net profit	£2023

She then put the net profit figure into the government calculator:

Budget for your Self Assessment tax bill if you're self-employed - GOV.UK (www.gov.uk)

Note: It is important to always use the tax calculator, and not estimate, as rates of tax and national insurance can and do change year to year, and you must have the up to date figure.

The calculator also caters for Scottish residents as the tax rates are different in Scotland.

The figures shown in Dianne's example are taken from the 2020-21 calculator!

This produced a required monthly provision for Dianne's tax and national insurance of £321.

She then inserted this figure, each month, into the cash flow forecast and arranged for the same sum to be transferred monthly to her business savings account. You can clearly see how this best practice will work for Dianne when the time comes for her to pay her tax and national insurance, as she will have put the funds aside.

First Time Cash flow Forecast extract—Fully Completed.

Income	Pre-start Up	MONTH 1	MONTH 2	MONTH 3
Income target		2300	2300	2300
	£0.00			
(A) Total Income	£0.00	£2,300.00	£2,300.00	£2,300.00

Expenditure	Pre-start Up	MONTH 1	MONTH 2	MONTH 3
Art materials		120	120	120
Business insurance		16	16	16
web hosting		11	11	11
Business mobile		30	30	30
Marketing		100	100	100
Diannes wage		1600	1600	1600
Provision for Tax & NI		321	321	321
(B) Total costs	£0.00	£2,198.00	£2,198.00	£2,198.00

You will see that to be able to set yourself a monthly target to aim for, having taken account of all your costs, is a very satisfying place to be in your first year of trade!

Let us now undertake a short analysis of the cash flow forecast as follows:

- Dianne has a monthly income target of £2300 to aim for knowing that she can cover all of her business expenses.
- She can pay herself a wage of £1600.
- She can meet her tax and national insurance commitments.
- At the end of each month, Dianne will have a surplus of £102.00 left in her business bank account if her income target is achieved (see line A – B).

Income	Pre-start Up	MONTH 1	MONTH 2	MONTH 3
Income target		2300	2300	2300
	£0.00			
(A) Total Income	£0.00	£2,300.00	£2,300.00	£2,300.00

Expenditure	Pre-start Up	MONTH 1	MONTH 2	MONTH 3
Art materials		120	120	120
Business insurance		16	16	16
web hosting		11	11	11
Business mobile		30	30	30
Marketing		100	100	100
Diannes wage		1600	1600	1600
Provision for Tax & NI		321	321	321
(B) Total costs	£0.00	£2,198.00	£2,198.00	£2,198.00
A - B	£0.00	£102.00	£102.00	£102.00
Balance B/Forward	£0.00	£0.00	£102.00	£204.00
Cash in the Business	£0.00	£102.00	£204.00	£306.00

Let's now move on to Dianne's costing and pricing calculations using the figures taken from the first time cash flow forecast.

Costing and pricing within the "first-time" cash flow forecast.

Dianne's costing and pricing calculations

Let us now return to Dianne's ideal self-employment model. You may remember that she wants to work three days a week giving art lessons.

We are now going to use the 'first-time' cash flow forecast to determine the pricing of her lessons now she has her monthly income target of £2300 to aim for.

The calculation is as follows:

First, Dianne needs to decide how many weeks in the year she will work.

She decides that she will take 3 weeks holiday and add a further week in case of potential illness. This means she is planning to work **48 weeks** in her first year.

- **Working her proposed 3 days per week** means that she has **12 days available each month to deliver** art classes.
- From Dianne's market research, she feels **she can comfortably deliver 2 art sessions each day**, therefore **in a month, she can deliver 24 art sessions.**
- To work out the **cost of each art session**, we take the **monthly income target of £2300 and divide this by 24** (which means she needs an income of **£96 per session**).
- Assuming **6 students per session** she will need to **charge £16 per student.**
- But **if that falls to 4** in any session, she will need to increase the **charge to £24 per student** to cover her costs.
- She could sell this to her students as she will have more time to spend with each of them.

Dianne now knows the **minimum** amount that she can charge for her basic sessions and the number she needs to deliver each month.

> ### Bluebell Tip
>
> When calculating your pricing using this method, you may wish to consider putting in place a contingency pricing strategy.
>
> When Dianne undertook her market research, her prospective customers gave her an idea of how much they would be prepared to pay for an art session. The range was between £30 and £40. Using this information, Dianne might, therefore, be wise to consider increasing her £16 to £24 minimum price for basic sessions across the year to cover any times where she is unable to fill a session.
>
> This contingency plan could be a 'lifesaver' for Dianne and could improve her income levels across the year. She could also earn more by running specialist courses from time to time.

Dianne now has a **steer** on her pricing, as she knows the minimum she needs to earn each month.

Understanding where our key business drivers sit within cash flow forecasts.

Three key business drivers and **two best-practice tactics** can be monitored via the cash flow forecast documents to aid your business knowledge and ongoing analysis.

These are:

1. Knowledge and regular analysis of cash flow forecasts – **Key Driver**.
2. Market Research – **Key Driver**, generates sales and feeds into the income line/income target (yellow).
3. Marketing – Sales & Service – **Key Driver**, generates sales and feeds into the income line/income target (yellow).
4. Proprietor's drawings calculated from Personal Survival Budget – **Best Practice** (pink).
5. Making provision to save to pay HMRC for tax & national insurance – **Best Practice** (turquoise).

The likelihood of your business being a success is entwined with how well you understand and manage all 5 key drivers.

The 'rule of thumb' here, as defined by Pareto (an economist) is that you spend 80% of your time on 20% of your activities.

Using that rule, by concentrating on the 5 key drivers, you will be working on those aspects of your business that have the biggest influence on your results for good, or for worse if you ignore them!

Introducing our Bluebell budget vs actual cash flow document.

The last cash flow document that we are going to look at is the budget versus actual cash flow forecast.

For an example of its layout please see the extract below:

	January		February		March	
INCOME	Budget	Actual	Budget	Actual	Budget	Actual
Business income	£0.00	£0.00	£0.00	£0.00	£0.00	£0.00
Loans	£0.00	£0.00	£0.00	£0.00	£0.00	£0.00
Grants	£0.00	£0.00	£0.00	£0.00		
Capital Introduced	£0.00	£0.00	£0.00	£0.00	£0.00	£0.00
(A) Total Income	£0.00	£0.00	£0.00	£0.00	£0.00	£0.00
Business Expenditure						
Stock Purchases	£0.00	£0.00	£0.00	£0.00	£0.00	£0.00
	£0.00	£0.00	£0.00	£0.00	£0.00	£0.00
Business Insurance	£0.00	£0.00	£0.00	£0.00	£0.00	£0.00
Business Mileage	£0.00	£0.00	£0.00	£0.00	£0.00	£0.00
Stationery and postage	£0.00	£0.00	£0.00	£0.00	£0.00	£0.00
Marketing	£0.00	£0.00	£0.00	£0.00	£0.00	£0.00
Web Hosting	£0.00	£0.00	£0.00	£0.00	£0.00	£0.00
Accountancy fees	£0.00	£0.00	£0.00	£0.00	£0.00	£0.00
	£0.00	£0.00	£0.00	£0.00	£0.00	£0.00
Provision for Tax and NI	£0.00	£0.00	£0.00	£0.00	£0.00	£0.00
Owners wage (Drawings)	£0.00	£0.00	£0.00	£0.00	£0.00	£0.00
	£0.00	£0.00	£0.00	£0.00	£0.00	£0.00
Loan repayments	£0.00	£0.00	£0.00	£0.00	£0.00	£0.00
Loan Interest	£0.00	£0.00	£0.00	£0.00	£0.00	£0.00
(B) Total Expenditure	£0.00	£0.00	£0.00	£0.00	£0.00	£0.00
(A-B)	£0.00	£0.00	£0.00	£0.00	£0.00	£0.00
Balance B/Forward	£0.00	£0.00	£0.00	£0.00	£0.00	£0.00
Cash in the business	£0.00	£0.00	£0.00	£0.00	£0.00	£0.00

This is the basic cash flow forecast but it is re-designed as a management analysis tool. It, therefore, has one key difference from the basic cash flow. You will see under each month that there are two headings, one **budget** and one **actual**. This allows the business owner to budget for what they expect will happen (as in the basic cash flow) and at the end of the month put against those figures the actual figures. This tool is, therefore, exceptionally powerful in terms of business analysis and decision-making.

How can it be used in the analysis?

The fact that you will be reviewing your figures every month means that you will be keeping your books up to date and staying close to your figures. This is beneficial for you as the business owner and will ensure that you will become more confident about your forecasting.

Each month as you add the actual figures to each subject line on the document, you will see how far away you are from your predicted figures. If there is a difference, and it is a small one, it will give you confidence that you are on track with your forecasts. However, you may find that your figures are outside your predictions, and it is then important to understand why.

If your figures are better than anticipated, you might be tempted to forgo the analysis, but it is essential that you understand where any differences have arisen. It may be that a supplier cheque has not been presented for payment, not that your sales income has improved, for example.

If your figures are widely out, it is obviously important that you understand why, and so, you will need to identify exactly where you have overstated or understated your predictions. It may be that sales have been better than anticipated, or that a payment due in a particular month hasn't arrived as expected.

Once identified, you should then re-forecast and fine-tune your predictions for the upcoming months, making the necessary adjustments. By doing this, you will have a much better understanding of what is happening in your business, and it will give you a vastly improved opportunity of making it a success.

Bluebell Tip

To help with this, we strongly recommend that you put all your business income through your business bank account so that you can undertake a thorough cash flow analysis against your business bank statement as all income and expenditure will be shown there.

In Chapter 5, we mentioned the Free Agent accounts software available free of charge for business customers (at the time of writing) with NatWest's business bank accounts. This software now includes

> a near term cash flow forecast as part of the package. As a month's accounts are inputted into the application, the app automatically calculates the near future cash flow. Great idea!

A simple best practice to a deeper understanding of cash flow

The key to really understanding cash flow forecasting is not to see this document as an isolated spreadsheet. A simple trick to enable a deeper understanding of cash flow is to imagine your business bank account sitting alongside the cash flow forecast and visualise the monthly income on the cash flow forecast physically being paid into your business bank account. Likewise, for the business expenses on the cash flow forecast coming out of the business bank account.

To illustrate this link between the cash flow forecast and the business bank account see the example below. It belongs to Hugo, and you will learn more about him below.

HUGO

Hugo is a self-employed gardener with four clients, Mr Crimes, Mr Belfield, Mr Cartwright and Mr Brown, each of whom pays him £500 for a week's gardening and landscaping work.

Earlier in this section, we learned about the budget/actual cash flow and the best practice of plotting the actual figures against the monthly predictions each month for you to make strategic business decisions.

To illustrate this link between the cash flow forecast and the business bank account, we have taken two months of Hugo's **actual** cash flow figures from the budget/actual cash flow forecast, showing **the actual figures on the left and the business bank account on the right** for you to visualise. This important best practice will aid a better understanding of cash flow.

Income	June (£)	July (£)
Gardening income	2000	2500
(A) Total Income	2000	2500
Business Expenditure		
Web hosting	11	11
Business insurance	16	16
Business mobile	32	32
Marketing	100	100
Petrol for mowers		48
Hugo's wage	1400	1400
Tax provision	268	399
(B) Total Business Expenditure	1827	2006
A - B	173	494
Bank balance brought forward from the end of the previous month	NIL	173
Cash in the business bank account at the end of the month	173	667

Description and date	Paid In	Paid Out	?
June 2020			
5th June Crimes bank transfer in	500		500 CR
9th June EE Mobile direct debit		32	468 CR
12th June Belfield bank transfer in	500		968 CR
15th June ABC Marketing standing order		100	868 CR
17th June web hosting direct debit		11	857 CR
19th June Cartwright bank transfer in	500		1357 CR
26th June Brown bank transfer in	500		1857 CR
30th June tax provision transfer to tax saving account		268	1589 CR
30th June Hugo's wage transfer to private account		1400	189 CR
30th June JPB Business Insurance direct debit		16	173 CR
July 2020			
3rd July Crimes bank transfer in	500		673 CR
9th July EE Mobile direct debit		32	641 CR
10th July Belfield bank transfer in	500		1141 CR
15th July ABC Marketing standing order		100	1041 CR
17th July web hosting direct debit		11	1030 CR
17th July Cartwright bank transfer in	500		1530 CR
18th July BP Garage petrol card payment		48	1482 CR
24th July Brown bank transfer in	500		1982 CR
30th July JPB Business Insurance direct debit		16	1966 CR
31st July Crimes bank transfer in	500		2466 CR
31st July Hugo's wage transfer to private account		1400	1066 CR
31st July tax provision transfer to tax saving account		399	667 CR

You now have three financial management tools to use which are essential to make your proposed business a success!

If you don't use them, your business will be less successful, as you will not get close enough to your finances to manage them appropriately.

You will only need to use the **'first-time' cash flow forecast** during the planning stage of your business. You will then recognise where the 5 key business drivers and the 2 best practice elements feed in, and this will help your understanding of how best to influence your results on your business journey.

The **basic cash flow forecast** should be used whenever you are producing figures for others, for example, your bank with grant applications, or for other stakeholders.

Finally, the **budget vs actual cash flow** will be used throughout your business journey. You will know your business and its financials thoroughly as a result.

> ### Bluebell Tip
>
> Of course, for those of you who will need to issue invoices, the best way to ensure that cash flows into your account, as required, is to ensure that you create an invoice as soon as a job of work has been completed. It is even better if you can take a deposit from your customer at the start of the job which will cover the cost of the materials. Be sure to advise your customer of the expected payment terms on the job estimate and show this on the invoice as well e.g., payment on job completion. If you can get into the habit of issuing invoices in this way, and follow up if payment is not made promptly, you will find your cash flow is much improved.
>
> Once you have decided on the software for your bookkeeping, you will receive prompts for any overdue invoices you have issued. Please ensure that you deal with them straight away!

As we discussed earlier, in our road map analogy, the cash flow forecast is the fuel gauge that ensures that you do not run out of 'fuel' on your business journey. This is a massive asset for any business owner, and you should take full advantage of the benefits it provides!

We will now look at getting your business up and running and cover the steps you need to take to achieve that.

CHAPTER 8

MAKE IT HAPPEN!

> **Bluebell Documents to Download for this Chapter**
> **Improvement Circle review worksheet**

Working through this book, you have had the opportunity to look closely at yourself and your business idea. You have learned ways to build on your strengths and limit any areas of weakness. You can take comfort from what you have discovered about yourself, and you will have learned which skills you need to obtain to become a successful entrepreneur.

You have also looked at all aspects of your proposed new business and researched it in great detail, and you will now know if you have a viable enterprise in your sights.

You will be disappointed if you do not, but it is better to find out now than after 12 months of trade and a substantial loss of time and money. This doesn't have to be the end of your start-up journey; you will just need to re-think and re-consider your options/products.

For those of you who now have a completed a road map for your business journey, let's look at what you need to do next to make it happen!

We promised you several links to provide you with a wealth of information to help you get your business 'up and running'. This way, if the requirements change, you will always have the most up to date information! Here they are:

Register your sole trader business.

First, you will need to advise HMRC that you are starting up a business.

You are classed as a sole trader if you start working for yourself. This means that you are self-employed.

You can be employed, and self-employed at the same time, for example, if you are running your business alongside working for an employer. Many entrepreneurs start up in this way so that they continue to receive a wage from their employment whilst they are building sales income in their new business.

A sole trader is responsible for running their business and for meeting the legal requirements that come with it. As a sole trader, you can keep your profits after tax; however, you are also personally responsible for any debts of your business. A sole trader can employ staff.

The government video and government link below, gives you guidance on how to register.

Set up as a sole trader - GOV.UK
Registering for Self-Assessment - YouTube HM Revenue & Customs

Tax Returns

When you start up your business as a sole trader, you will be expected to advise HMRC of any profits you earn by way of an annual self-assessment tax return.

Learn about how to register, timeframes and deadlines below.

The government links below give guidance on how to complete a self-assessment tax return.

How to register for Self Assessment.GOV.UK
Self-Assessment tax returns – GOV.UK

National Insurance

As a self-employed person, and if you are below state pension age, you will have to pay national insurance contributions if your profits are in excess of the current government annual thresholds. Payment of national insurance qualifies you for certain benefits including a state pension.

You will pay class 2 and class 4 national insurance.

As learned in chapter 7, you can calculate your projected self-assessment tax and national insurance class 2 & class 4 contributions by using the government calculator. You will pay your national insurance at the same time as your tax via your annual self-assessment return.

The government links below offer guidance.

National Insurance – GOV.UK
Self-Assessment tax calculator - GOV.UK

It is also worth knowing that you may be able to make voluntary class 3 national insurance payments to fill any gaps in your contribution history to qualify for benefits like a state pension.

If this applies to you please have a look at the link below:

Class 3 Voluntary National Insurance - GOV.UK

How to Calculate your Taxable Profits

Please see chapter 7.
The government links below give guidance.

What expenses can I include in my Self-Assessment tax return? - GOV.UK
How to Calculate your Taxable Profits GOV.UK

Capital Allowances

When you buy assets for your business and keep them in your business e.g., equipment, machinery, and business vehicles, you can claim capital allowances. You can deduct some or all of the value of the item from your profits before you pay tax.

The government link below offers guidance.
https://startupbusinessplanning.co.uk/ebooks#book1links

Construction Industry

If you are looking to set up a business in the construction industry please read this government link for guidance:

Construction Industry Scheme - Gov.UK

Bookkeeping/Records

You must keep records of your business transactions if you are self-employed as a sole trader.
The government video and government link below offer guidance.

Self-Employed Records GOV.UK
How long to keep your self employed records - GOV.UK

Other Business Structures

This book has been written for sole traders to keep the content simple, focused, and effective. However, there are a number of other legal entities which you may wish to consider.

The government video and government link below offer guidance on how to register.

I'm registering my business - which structure should I choose? – HMRC YouTube

Choosing the right business structure – Companies House

VAT

What is VAT?

Value-added tax (VAT) is a tax that is levied on the price of a product or service. It is a complex subject and there are a number of different schemes available to businesses. We reiterate what we said in Chapter 7 that it is important for you to speak to an accountant regarding your financial situation and seek advice on whether VAT is applicable (when you have to register) or beneficial (when you can voluntarily register) to your business.

The government video and government link below provide guidance.

Do I need to register my business for VAT? - YouTube – GOV.UK
VAT Registration - GOV.UK

Raising Business Finance

If you need to raise finance for your business, there are a number of options available:

Friends and Family

Please don't take your loved ones for granted. If they are good enough to support you in your business venture, ensure that you put the agreement on a business footing by writing everything down and seeking legal advice where necessary.

A simple, signed agreement between both parties will make matters clear between you and will help if there are any problems down the line.

Start-Up Loans/Grants

The UK Government puts aside a proportion of taxpayers' money each year to put towards business grants and funding new enterprise.

The money is distributed through local and national organisations that you apply for, and they will decide if you are eligible for funding.

The government links below give guidance:

https://www.gov.uk/apply-start-up-loan
for
Finance and Support your business - GOV.UK

Banks

Approaching a bank is the traditional method of raising finance for a new business. In addition to the 'big four' long-established banks, there are a number of 'new kids on the block'. Have a look at their start-up offerings and decide which best suits you.

If you already have a personal bank account, you may find it helpful to open your business account with the same bank too. They will already know you and you can easily manage your finances.

Angel Investors

This is where investors use their own money to invest in a business and will normally take shares in return. They will invest their own time, expertise and money in your business and will expect to get a return in 3/5 years. You may have watched 'Dragons Den' on TV. This is how they invest in new businesses.

There are a number of websites that bring together angel investors and entrepreneurs

Angel Investment - British Business Bank

Crowdfunding

Many people are looking for new ways to invest their money and are interested in crowdfunding for businesses. This is where a large number of people would each invest a small amount of money in your enterprise.

There are various forms of crowdfunding, donation, equity and debt and you can find out more at The UK Crowdfunding Association (UKCFA)

https://www.ukcfa.org.uk

> **Insurance**
>
> All business owners should consider protecting themselves and their assets from unexpected events and business risks by taking out insurance.
> **Certain insurances are required by law e.g., if you take on employees or drive a vehicle for your business, you must be insured. It is, therefore, important that you make yourself fully aware of all the requirements!**
> Before starting up, we recommend that you speak to an independent insurance broker to get a tailored quote.
> Most banks can introduce you to their recommended brokers too, or they may have a specially designed insurance package for businesses.
> In addition, many insurers will allow you to pay your premium by monthly payments but that may cost slightly more than if you can pay in full upfront.

Now that we have looked at the formalities that you need to consider so that you can get your business up and running, we will look into the future of your new business.

Continuous Improvement

Getting your business underway is just the very start of your business journey; you not only want to succeed but you want to constantly improve so you must get into the habit of continuous improvement.

What is this? Well, it is a means of continuing to review your business plans once your business is up and running.

For you to achieve this, we have developed the
IMPROVEMENT CIRCLE:

Improvement Circle Review

Review Plans
1. Review
2. Revise
3. Plan
4. Action

Arrows: Business Planning, Cashflow Forecasting, Market Research, Marketing - Sales and Service, Personal Character SWOC

Bluebell Business

This is a very, simple concept but will make a massive difference to your business. The idea is that once your business has started up and your plans are live that you start to validate and test them by **overlaying** the improvement circle on each of the key drivers.

You will see that the **key business drivers** are indicated by the arrows:

Business Planning
Market Research
Marketing – Sales & Customer Service
Personal Character & Skills Analysis (SWOC)
Cashflow Forecasting

The improvement circle should be used regularly with these 5 key drivers but is equally effective when overlaid on the smaller component parts that make up these key drivers. For example, within the

Marketing – Sales and Customer Service key driver, the improvement circle could be used with a specific marketing sales tactic.

You will remember that 20% of your business activities are responsible for producing 80% of your profits. So, if you continually review and improve upon these key elements, that will drive your success.

Let's overlay the circle on market research as an example. You have decided on your 2/3 key customer groups, and you have your avatars as a reference point. You have also mystery shopped your competitors. However, matters can change quickly in business with new products, fashion trends, and services popping up regularly. So, it is important to regularly review your plans—the improvement circle is an ideal tool to use.

You will see that the Improvement Circle Review has 4 stages:

1. **Review** – This is the important stage. Review your plans. See what is working and what is not. Many entrepreneurs don't think of this and miss emerging trends or fail to recognise that they are working with a customer group that is not the ideal one for them, going forward.

2. **Revise** – Consider new (hopefully more successful) tactics, whether these relate to customer groups, your product or service, or emerging trends, etc. Also, consider whether your implementation has been as strong as you would have liked. This is the point that you will tweak your plan to make it better!

3. **Plan** – Decide how to deliver your new plan (full and thorough planning is essential at this stage).

4. **Action** – Start to action the revised plan.

The Improvement Circle is designed like this, so the process of reviewing and planning is ongoing . The time distance between these reviews will depend very much upon you and your business, and the key driver or tactic you are considering. We would recommend that you review your new plans after two to three months to check progress and if all is well look again after six or twelve months. We would recommend that you review your research annually as a minimum. You can download the Improvement Circle Review Worksheet here or from the start of the chapter.

You will then be continually improving both yourself (via the review of your personal character SWOC), and your business, via regular reviews of the other key drivers which strongly influence your business.

This is important, as it is extremely easy to let your time be taken up by working 'in' your business, rather than working 'on' your business. You may have heard of this phrase. What it is telling you is that it is easy to get swamped with minor day to day activities that contribute little to your business success. Whereas becoming structured and ensuring that you are spending time on the key areas which are the foundations of your business will help to drive your profits.

Let's think about our road map analogy:

The Improvement Circle review is the steering wheel that gets you from A to B. If you are going in the wrong direction (i.e., away from profit) you have the opportunity, with regular improvement circle reviews, to turn your 'vehicle' in the right direction. The five key drivers are the gears that link together to start and keep your vehicle (business) moving. Imagine your business journey without these checks, it will definitely be down to chance rather than good planning!

We said that we would keep our advice simple, focused, and effective and we hope that we have achieved that!

All that is left to say is that we wish you every success with your new business and hope that you enjoy the satisfaction that building a profitable business by your own efforts brings!

It's time to go and 'Make it Happen'!

Printed in Great Britain
by Amazon